The
Housing Act
1988

by Les Burrows

revised edition

Shelter
NATIONAL CAMPAIGN FOR THE HOMELESS

ACKNOWLEDGEMENTS

I would like to thank the following people for sparing the time to answer my questions, give their comments on drafts of this Guide, or who have allowed me to look at drafts of their own —

Janet Briscoe, Sheila Camp, Russell Campbell, Alison Crisp, Mike England, Danny Friedman, John Goodwin, Ed Jankowski, Joe Oldman, Mike Reardon, Matthew Shaps, Paul Walentowicz and Steve Wilcox.

I would also like to thank all the people — far too numerous to mention here — who were involved with me in trying to influence the policies in this Act when it was a Bill, for without them this Guide would not have been possible so soon after enactment. Any omissions or errors are the author's alone.

This Guide is not a legal textbook: simplifications have been necessary in an attempt to make a complex piece of legislation accessible and useful to as wide an audience as possible.

This second edition takes account of the numerous Regulations and Circulars relating to the Act, issued up to May 1989. It also attempts to improve on the first edition. My thanks to all those who helped with this.

Les Burrows
June 1989

Contents

3. Housing Action Trusts

4. Change of landlord — public sector

5. Other issues

6. Conclusions

Introduction

THIS ACT, WHICH IS CONCERNED with **rented** housing, is an important element in the Government's overall privatisation policy. The belief behind this policy is that the system of public housing provision and management is bankrupt, and that private money and management is the key to the future. The intention therefore is that the private sector should have an increasing role in the provision of new homes, and control over existing homes wherever possible. At the same time the Government has adopted the housing association movement as the means of blurring the distinctions between private and public provision.

The Act's provisions concerning rights and responsibilities have been tailored accordingly. In general this has meant a weakening of tenancy rights, and a corresponding weakening of landlord responsibilities. But it is not just a question of a clash of opinion as to which policy will provide homes for the future. There is also a strong element of brimstone in this legislation. The Government really does believe that tenants have fallen victim to what William Waldegrave, who ceased to be Minister of Housing half way through passage of the Act, called the "dread drug of dependency," and a wide range of social policies have been revised with this belief in mind.

1. Private renting

INTRODUCTION

At the turn of the century the private rented sector dominated Britain's housing. The scandal of widespread bad housing conditions within that sector led to public health Acts and then housing and rent Acts which attempted to deal with the 19th Century legacy of slums and exploitation. Local authorities were believed to be the future rented housing providers; and around the same time the rise of the building society movement placed owner-occupation within the reach of more and more people. The private landlord, dependent on profit, unwilling to accept constraints which were an increasing requirement of modern housing provision and management, began to fade away. The sector continues to decline to this day. Today it accounts for only just over 7% of the country's housing.

There has been a great deal of legislation this century targeted on private renting. In essence it has covered security of tenure, rent, and the physical condition of the property. Battles have raged long and hard. The battle lines have been drawn between on the one hand, those who take the view that social requirements demand security of tenure, rents which really are within tenants' means, and strong rights and duties concerning conditions; and, on the other hand, those who take the view that such controls merely put the private landlord out of business — which does not help the cause of tenants. The argument of this latter group is that if controls are taken off the private landlord will provide the housing.

However, the history of decontrol has not been one of increased supply. Before this Act the last major decontrolling legislation was the 1957 Rent Act. In its wake more homes left the sector than ever before, and it helped give rise to a phenomenon which has haunted the decontrollers ever since, and will continue to do so — Rachmanism. Rents rose dramatically, and there was an epidemic of eviction and homelessness.

Decontrol did not work in 1957, and it will not work in 1989. The reason is simple — the decline of private renting has been brought about by changes in the financial infrastructure, including the treatment given to the dominant part of the private housing sector, owner-occupation. Registration of rents, security of tenure, and other controls are not root causes. The Government cannot avoid the simple truth — the rents demanded by landlords to persuade them to stay in letting are far beyond the means of the great majority of potential tenants.

In our view the 1988 Housing Act will lead to a smaller not a larger sector. Six month assured shortholds will be the dominant face of new letting — with eviction and homelessness at the end. There will be a disastrous gap between the help people get from housing benefit and the rent they actually have to pay — which will also lead to eviction and homelessness. A housing regime based on fewer rights for new tenants means that pre–1988 Act tenants, although still protected by the Rent Act 1977, will be more vulnerable to landlord ambitions — leading to more harassment and illegal eviction. Job mobility, by which the Government has placed great store, will be actively hindered by this Act, for movement will seize up in a climate of decreased supply and unaffordable rents. In general, as the Act tightens its grip fewer people will be able to gain access to the sector, and those who have gained access will find it difficult to remain within it. A smaller 'traditional private landlord' sector will come into being, occupied by well-off tenants, but the reality of life for tenants on low or average incomes will be the denial of a proper home.

1.1 NEW FORMS OF TENANCY FOR NEW LETS

FROM 15TH JANUARY 1989 landlords have been able to let on the basis of "assured" tenure, and the related "assured shorthold" tenure.

In general landlords are not able to let on the basis of Rent Act protected tenancies. There are a few exceptions:

a) the contract was entered into before 15th January 1989;
b) immediately beforehand the tenant was a protected or statutory tenant of the same landlord (see 1.3 for more details); or
c) it is ordered as such by a county court as suitable alternative accommodation. The qualifying conditions for assured tenancies under the 1980 Housing Act will cease to have effect. (These were a landlord approval system; the specification of money to be spent on works; basic fitness standard to apply before letting; and the removal of approved body status from landlords.) Existing pre-1988 Act assured tenancies (under the 1980

Housing Act) will become assured tenancies under this Act unless the tenant has applied for a new tenancy which has not yet been granted.

Existing pre-1988 Act assured tenancies can only be specifically excluded from being assured tenancies under this Act if they are Crown tenancies or public sector tenancies, or if they are tenancies which are continuing as a result of an application for a new tenancy under section 24 of the 1954 Landlord and Tenant Act, or as a result of any provision of Part IV of that Act.

Otherwise a letting is excluded from being an assured tenancy in a number of circumstances:
● tenancies contracted before January 15th 1989;
● the first 12 months after the tenant has received notification of tenancies granted by other bodies in relation to local authorities' temporary housing duties under the homelessness legislation, specifically where inquiries are pending, intentional homelessness decisions, and referral to another authority. These are contained in the 1985 Housing Act Section 64(1) (decision on homelessness or threatened homelessness) or 68(3) (which authority has a duty to rehouse) of the 1985 Housing Act. The rule which already applies to the 1985 Housing Act secure tenancy regime is now reproduced for the assured tenancy regime. A local authority can ask another body to house a homeless household temporarily in order to meet its statutory duties in the three circumstances above, and an assured tenancy will not arise during the 12 months, even after a local authority has accepted a full duty to secure rehousing;
● tenancies where the rateable value is more than £1,500 in Greater London, or £750 elsewhere;
● no rent is payable, or the rent is less than two-thirds the rateable value;
● business tenancies;
● licensed premises;
● tenancies let with more than two acres of agricultural land;
● an agricultural holding lived in by the person(s) in control of farming the holding;
● lettings to students by a specified educational institution;
● holiday lets;
● where the landlord is resident;
● Crown tenancies;
● public sector tenancies (including councils, HATS, and fully mutual housing cooperatives);
● transitional cases (secure, protected, housing association, and Rent (Agriculture) Act tenancies).

It has been suggested that because of wording variations between Sections 1 and 3 of the 1988 Housing Act the exclusions listed above would not apply in cases where a tenant shares accommodation but has exclusive use of a bedroom — in other words, that in some circumstances people in shared accommodation would have more rights than people who were not sharing. However, we are advised that even though the Act may be badly drafted in terms of the relationship between these two Sections, this is not its effect. The list of exclusions applies in all cases.

1.2 EXISTING TENANTS STILL PROTECTED BY THE RENT ACT

EXISTING TENANTS PROTECTED UNDER the 1977 Rent Act (a regulated tenancy) will keep their protection during that tenancy, whether or not there is a current registered rent. They will still have Rent Act security of tenure. They will still be able to go to the Rent Officer to have a "fair rent" registered. But the 1988 Housing Act (with effect from January 15th 1989) repeals the power of local authorities to apply to a Rent Officer on a tenant's behalf.

If after January 15th 1989 ownership of a property let on a fully protected 1977 Rent Act tenancy (a regulated tenancy) passes to a housing association, a housing trust, the Housing Corporation, or Housing for Wales, the Act allows these bodies to continue the letting on the basis of fair rent registration covered by the 1977 Rent Act, and security of tenure covered by the 1985 Housing Act. This in effect means no loss of rights.

1.3 EXISTING PROTECTED TENANTS' RIGHTS FOLLOWING A MOVE

AFTER JANUARY 15TH 1989 if an existing tenant who is already fully protected by the 1977 Rent Act is offered alternative accommodation by their landlord — either in the same house, or in another house the landlord owns — that tenancy cannot be an assured tenancy or an assured shorthold tenancy. It will be a regulated tenancy under the 1977 Rent Act if it falls within that Act's definition of a regulated tenancy. But tenants should not sign anything without getting advice, because some landlords may try to give less security, and thereby take rights away from tenants.

If the landlord goes to court to seek possession of the tenant's home, and offers an assured tenancy as suitable alternative accommodation, the county court has to decide whether this tenancy gives the equivalent security to the regulated tenancy — if it thinks it does not then it can direct that the tenant will get a 1977 Rent Act regulated tenancy.

1.4 SECURITY OF TENURE

A. ASSURED TENANCIES

Assured tenancies can be **periodic** (such as weekly or monthly), or **fixed-term** (the Act does not specify a minimum or maximum term).

An assured tenancy does not depend on there being a written agreement. However, Section 5 of the 1985 Landlord and Tenant Act applies — information to be contained in Rent Books. If the assured tenancy is weekly then a weekly rent book will be required, which will have to set out details of how the rent is payable.

To evict a periodic tenant a landlord will first have to give the tenant a written "Notice Seeking Possession" (NOSP). Statutory Instrument 1988 No. 2203, which came into force on January 15th 1989, sets out this prescribed form. It cannot be used for assured shorthold tenants or for assured agricultural occupants. It is Form No. 3 — Notice Seeking Possession of a Property Let on an Assured Tenancy. This causes some confusion, because the Act itself refers to Notice of Proceedings for Possession. In other words, to be accurate we now have to refer to it as a NOSP, not a NOPP (as we called it in the first edition of this Guide). It will have to state the details of the claim, as well as the Ground(s) for possession the landlord is using. It is not a Notice to Quit (a procedure not useable under the assured and assured shorthold system). The court order ends the tenancy, not the NOSP. The NOSP will be 2 weeks or 2 months depending on the ground used. After the NOSP has been served the landlord has up to 12 months to ask the county court to make a possession order. In the case of some grounds for possession the court has discretion to refuse a possession order — that is to say the tenant has a defence.

To evict the tenant when a fixed-term assured tenancy comes to an end the landlord has to serve a NOSP and satisfy the court that there is a ground for possession. The landlord can also serve a NOSP during the fixed-term tenancy if s/he alleges that the tenant has breached the contract, and if the contract entitles the landlord to end it.

There are two basic types of Ground — **mandatory**, where the county court must order possession if the Ground is proven; and **discretionary,** where the court **has the power** to refuse an order, even if the Ground is proven, if it thinks an order would be unreasonable.

MANDATORY GROUNDS FOR POSSESSION

GROUND 1. The landlord, whose only or principal home it once was, wants the tenant to leave, OR if it was bought before the tenancy began, and the landlord wants the accommodation for him/herself or spouse to live in as their only or principal home. [2 months NOSP]

GROUND 2. The landlord has defaulted on a mortgage granted before the tenancy began, and the mortgagee (e.g. a bank or a building society) wants vacant possession in order to sell the property. [2 months NOSP]

GROUND 3. The tenancy is a fixed-term out of season let of no more than 8 months, where the property had been let for holiday purposes at some time during the preceding 12 months. [2 weeks NOSP]

GROUND 4. The tenancy is a fixed-term let of no more than 12 months, where the property had been let as a student letting at some time during the preceding 12 months. [2 weeks NOSP]

GROUND 5. The accommodation is held for the purpose of being available for occupation by a Minister of Religion, and the court is satisfied that it is now needed for that purpose. [2 months NOSP]

GROUND 6. This is what is known as the redevelopment Ground. [2 months NOSP]

It can be used where the landlord has owned the property since before the tenancy began, and intends to demolish or reconstruct all or a substantial part of the accommodation, or to carry out substantial works on it or on other parts of the building. It can also be used when the landlord who intends to redevelop has granted a lease to a registered housing association or a charitable housing trust, which has sublet to the tenant. It cannot be used where the assured tenant is a successor to a Rent Act tenant.

The landlord has to show that the work cannot reasonably be carried out without the tenant leaving, and evidence has to be given that:
a) the tenant will not agree to changes in the tenancy terms to give the landlord "such access and other facilities" to allow the intended work to be carried out; or
b) the nature of the intended work makes such variation impracticable; or
c) the tenant refuses to accept an assured tenancy of a reduced part of the accommodation, to enable the landlord to carry out the intended work on

the rest and have "access and other facilities" over the reduced part; or
d) the nature of the intended work makes a tenancy impracticable.

If a public sector tenant becomes an assured tenant under the "Tenants' Choice" scheme, or under a "voluntary transfer" arrangement, Ground 6 can be utilised if the new landlord has owned the accommodation since before the assured tenancy began. In practice, this means that the incoming landlord will not be able to use Ground 6, because it acquires its interest in the accommodation at the point at which an existing secure tenant becomes an assured tenant, not before the assured tenancy began.

GROUND 7. Where the tenant has a periodic tenancy (e.g. weekly, fortnightly, or monthly) and has it through a will or intestacy. But to use this Ground the landlord has to start court proceedings within 12 months of the former tenant's death (or a later date decided by the court if the landlord only later became aware of the death). Acceptance of rent after the former tenant's death does not create a new tenancy, unless the landlord has given written agreement to a different rent or some other change in tenancy terms. Ground 7 does not apply where a spouse succeeds to an assured periodic tenancy under Section 17 of the Act. [2 months NOSP]

GROUND 8. This is known as the "3 months' arrears" Ground. It can be used where 3 months' rent is unpaid (where rent is payable monthly); where one quarter's rent is more than 3 months in arrears (where rent is payable quarterly); where at least 3 months' rent is more than three months in arrears (where rent is payable yearly); or where at least 13 weeks' rent is in arrears (where rent is payable weekly or fortnightly). The important point to note is that these amounts of rent have to be unpaid both when the Notice Seeking Possession (NOSP) is served on the tenant, and on the actual court possession hearing date. [2 weeks NOSP]

DISCRETIONARY GROUNDS FOR POSSESSION

GROUND 9. Where suitable alternative accommodation is available for the tenant or will be when the possession order takes effect. [2 months NOSP]

Neither an assured shorthold tenancy, nor an assured tenancy subject to Grounds 1 to 5, can be suitable alternative accommodation — unless the present tenancy matches them. Possession can also be granted where the local housing authority gives a certificate saying that it will provide suitable alternative accommodation by a specific date. Part III of Schedule 2 to the Act sets out other conditions concerning suitability.

GROUND 10. Where there are any rent arrears on the date the Notice Seeking Possession (NOSP) is served on the tenant AND on the date the court summons is issued. [2 weeks NOSP]

GROUND 11. Where the tenant has "persistently delayed" paying rent — even though there may be no arrears at the date the court summons is issued. [2 weeks NOSP]

GROUND 12. Where there has been a breach of a tenancy obligation (other than one related to rent). [2 weeks NOSP]

GROUND 13. Where there has been a deterioration in the condition of the accommodation (or of any common parts) — caused by the tenant (or someone in the tenant's household); or if caused by a lodger or a sub-tenant the Ground can be used against the tenant if the tenant has not taken steps to get that person out. [2 weeks NOSP]

GROUND 14. Where the tenant (or someone in the tenant's household) "has been guilty of conduct which is a nuisance or annoyance" to adjoining occupiers; or has been convicted of using the accommodation or allowing it to be used "for immoral or illegal purposes." [2 weeks NOSP]

GROUND 15. Where furniture (if provided) has deteriorated due to ill-treatment by the tenant, household members etc (as in Ground 13). [2 weeks NOSP]

GROUND 16. Where the letting was in consequence of employment by the present or a previous landlord, and the tenant is no longer in that employment. [2 months NOSP]

NOTES ON GROUNDS:

A: To use Grounds 1 and 2 the landlord has to have served a notice on the tenant "not later than the beginning of the tenancy" that the Ground may be used. But the county court can decide to dispense with this requirement if it is "just and equitable" to do so.

B: Normally, before taking county court action, the landlord will have to give the tenant a written Notice Seeking Possession (NOSP). HOWEVER Section 8 of the Act says that where such a notice has not been served the county court can decide that it is "just and equitable" for it to be dispensed with — but a NOSP will always be required for Ground 8.

C: Landlords who obtain possession under Ground 6 or Ground 9 have to pay the tenant's reasonable removal expenses (Clause 11).

D: There are special rules for **fixed-term** assured tenancies.
a) The county court cannot grant a possession order to take effect during a fixed-term tenancy, under Grounds 1, 3, 4, 5, 6, 7, 9, or 16. And it can only grant an order under Grounds 2, 8, 10, 11, 12, 13, 14, or 15 if the tenancy agreement contains a provision saying that the Ground in question can be used.

E: The county court has power to adjourn proceedings, stay or suspend execution of an order, or postpone the date of possession — for as long as it likes. But it only has these powers under the Act in the case of the discretionary Grounds (i.e. 9 to 16).

In the case of the mandatory grounds the court may have the power to grant short adjournments under the 1984 County Courts Act.

F: If a landlord gets a possession order on any of these Grounds through "misrepresentation or concealment of material facts", the court has power to order the landlord to pay compensation to the former tenant.

G: The landlord cannot get a possession order on living accommodation the tenant shares with other people unless possession is also obtained on exclusively occupied separate accommodation. The county court can agree to a landlord's request to stop the tenant using all or any shared accommodation (as long as it is not living accommodation); or the tenant's right to use it — even by varying the number of other people having a right to use it. But the court order should not go further than what is allowed under the terms of the tenancy.

H: Court proceedings cannot be started later than 1 year after service of the NOSP.

B. ASSURED SHORTHOLD TENANCIES

An assured shorthold tenancy is an assured tenancy subject to certain rules, the main one being that the landlord can get possession at the end of a fixed-term. A tenancy cannot be a shorthold if it has been granted to a person who immediately before the grant was a (non-shorthold) assured tenant of the same landlord (i.e. in the same, or another building).

For an assured shorthold tenancy to be valid the landlord has to give the tenant a written notice (in proper form) before the tenancy begins, saying that it is a shorthold.

SI 1988 No. 2203 sets out the prescribed Form which must be used for this purpose. It is Form No. 7 — Notice of an Assured Shorthold Tenancy. This notice is used by the landlord before the tenancy is granted. It relates to Section 20 of the 1988 Housing Act.

Assured shorthold tenants do not have security of tenure. Shortholds are fixed-term lets (6 months minimum, no maximum).

To evict the tenant at the end of the shorthold (or during it if the landlord alleges that the tenant has breached the contract) the landlord can go to the county court. The court must make a possession order, as long as the tenant has been given 2 months written notice to quit at some time during the fixed-term. There is no prescribed form for this notice. Prescribed Form No. 3 (set out in SI 1988 No. 2203) which is for use concerning assured tenancies states specifically that it is not to be used in the case of an assured shorthold tenancy. No grounds for possession are needed other than that it is a shorthold.

If the landlord does nothing at all, the tenant stays on under a statutory periodic tenancy, and although a two months written NOSP is needed before the landlord can go to the county court for a possession order, the landlord can rely on a NOSP which has been given already during the fixed-term itself, rather than having to give a further notice. However, a further NOSP would have to be given if a new fixed-term assured shorthold was created, or if a new periodic tenancy came into being to replace the statutory periodic tenancy.

The notice must end no earlier than the last day of a period of the tenancy (e.g. if the tenancy runs from Saturday to Friday, it would have to end at the earliest on the Friday). The landlord can serve the tenant with a notice saying that it will not be a shorthold.

Alternatively, the landlord can give the tenant further shortholds (without having to serve a notice beforehand saying that it is a shorthold).

If a tenancy agreement contains a "break clause" — under which the landlord claims to be able to end the tenancy before the end of 6 months — it cannot be an assured shorthold (except where there has been a specific breach of contract). But this restriction only applies during the first 6 months the tenant is there. It should be noted that if the landlord does end the tenancy before the end of the fixed-term, for reasons of breach of contract, then in order to evict s/he still has to apply to the county court for a possession order, and in doing so still has to rely on one or more of the 1988 Housing Act's grounds for possession — as the ending of the contract does not dispense with the need to adhere to the Act's repossession requirements.

An assured tenancy with an agreement which contains a "break clause" will still be an assured tenancy. It cannot be a shorthold.

If an assured shorthold tenant wishes to end the tenancy before the fixed-term ends there is no absolute bar to the tenant doing so — as long as the tenancy agreement says it can be done. If however there is no permissive entitlement the tenant could try to persuade the landlord to agree to a surrender of the fixed-term agreement by mutual agreement. If this is not possible, and the tenant leaves before the fixed-term ends the position is somewhat complicated. If the landlord were to take court action against the tenant, in effect to sue for rent outstanding to the end of the fixed-term, the court would expect the landlord to "mitigate the loss" by making reasonable attempts to find a replacement tenant.

If the tenancy agreement does allow the tenant to break the fixed-term there still remains the question of what notice the tenant has to give. The answer is that it will be however long the agreement says it has to be. The essential point is that the tenant's break-clause is exactly that, and it stands as it is, for the fact that the assured shorthold tenancy is a fixed-term means that there cannot be a notice to quit as such.

1.5 ASSURED AND ASSURED SHORTHOLD TENANCY RENTS

THE BASIC IDEA BEHIND the Act is that landlords of new lets should be as free as possible to charge market rents, especially at the beginning of a tenancy.

A. WHERE THE TENANT HAS NO RIGHT TO GET A RENT DETERMINED

Assured and assured shorthold tenants will not be able to go to the Rent Officer to register a 'fair rent'. Instead, the Rent Assessment Committee (RAC) will take on the rent registration role, and will set its version of a market rent. But in the following circumstances the landlord has a free hand, because the RAC has no power to determine a rent.

ASSURED TENANCIES
● during a fixed term tenancy, or during the first year of a contractual periodic tenancy — and only afterwards if a notice of increase has been served;
● where the contract (oral or written) of a periodic tenancy has a provision for rent increases.

ASSURED SHORTHOLD TENANCIES
● during any second or later fixed-term tenancy;
● where no notice of increase has been served during a statutory periodic tenancy following on from a first fixed-term;
● where the Rent Assessment Committee decides there is an insufficient number of assured or assured shorthold tenancies in the locality, or that the rent payable is not significantly higher than the rent which the landlord could reasonably expect to get under assured or assured shorthold tenancies in the locality.

B. WHERE THE TENANT DOES HAVE A RIGHT TO GET A RENT SET

ASSURED TENANCIES

The landlord can increase the rent at the end of a fixed-term tenancy; or, at the end of the first year of a periodic tenancy where there is no rent review clause in the contract. And in these circumstances the tenant has a right to go to the RAC.

But to obtain a rent increase the landlord first has to serve the tenant with a written notice (which has to be in a proper form, prescribed by regulations) setting out the proposed new rent.

Form No. 1 — "Notice Proposing Different Terms for Statutory Periodic Tenancy" — can be given by a landlord to a tenant, or vice versa. It relates to Section 6(2) of the 1988 Housing Act. It is for use concerning proposed changes to non-rent tenancy terms, although it contains a section relating to a proposal for a rent increase consequent on the changed terms. The form is for use for tenancies which follow on from fixed-term assured tenancies. The RAC is not involved at this stage.

Form No. 5 is the landlord's "Notice Proposing a New Rent Under An Assured Periodic Tenancy or Agricultural Occupancy." This is the notice given by a landlord to a tenant to propose a new rent. It relates to Section 13(2) of the 1988 Housing Act. It can also be used to propose a new rent or licence fee for an assured agricultural occupancy. The RAC is not involved at this stage.

At least one month's notice has to be given. If the period of the tenancy is longer than one month, the period of notice should reflect the length of the tenancy — up to 6 months for a yearly tenancy. The new rent cannot take effect earlier than one year after the tenancy began (unless it is a statutory periodic tenancy) or the first anniversary of a previous increase.

Unless the landlord and the tenant agree a different rent, or the tenant goes to the RAC, the new rent takes effect on the date given in the notice. But any RAC referral must take place before the date stated in the notice.

The RAC has to abide by certain rules. While in general it has to set what it considers to be an open market rent, it has to disregard three elements: the fact that there is a sitting tenant; any improvements carried out by the tenant, where these have not been the result of an obligation to the landlord; and any failure by the tenant to honour the terms of the tenancy. It also has to take into account any notice served on the tenant prior to the beginning of the tenancy that indicates mandatory possession Grounds 1 to 5 may be used.

RAC rents are separate from service charges and rates.

In cases where the RAC has been asked to look at rents and other tenancy terms, the other terms have to be dealt with first.

RAC rents come into effect on the date in the landlord's notice, unless the RAC decides a later date is necessary because the earlier date would cause hardship to the tenant.

If landlords and assured tenants agree, not necessarily in writing, the RAC rent will not be the maximum chargeable.

The RAC can, but does not have to, carry on with a determination of a rent, if both the landlord and the tenant ask them not to.

The President of each RAC has to keep a public register of information relating to the assured tenancy, assured shorthold tenancy, and assured agricultural occupancy rents the RAC has determined.

SI 1988 No. 2199, which came into force on January 15th 1989, specifies this information, the manner in which it is to be made available, and the fee to be charged for the supply of a certified copy of such information. Although there is no charge for simply inspecting the information, RACs can charge £1 per determination for copies (or £1 per application where no determination has resulted).

SI 1988 No.2200, which came into force on January 15th 1989, amends the 1971 RAC regulations to take account of new functions under the 1988 Act. Under this amendment the RAC, following an application, has to serve a notice on the landlord and the tenant giving at least 7 days from the date of its service for written or oral representations to be made. The notice to the party who was not the applicant has to be accompanied by a copy of the application. In order for oral representations to be made the 7 day limit can be extended. They can be made by a barrister, a solicitor or a lay person.

The RAC can make any inquiry it wants to, and SI 1988 No. 2203, which came into force on January 15th 1989, contains the form it has to use:- Form No. 9 — Notice by Rent Assessment Committee Requiring Further Information.

The RAC has power to insist that a landlord or a tenant provides information "reasonably required." Failure to provide it is a criminal offence punishable by a maximum £400 fine. (This is level 3 on the scale of fines, and has not changed since 1984.)

SI 1988 No. 2203 also sets out other forms to be used in relation to RAC determination of assured tenancy rents. The first is Form No. 2 — Application Referring a Notice Under Section 6(2) to a Rent Assessment Committee. This is the form used by a landlord or a tenant where there is a dispute following service of Form No. 1 above. It can also be used where there was an earlier assured agricultural occupancy. The second is Form No. 6 — Application Referring a Notice Proposing A New Rent Under An Assured Periodic Tenancy or Agricultural Occupancy to a Rent Assessment Committee. This is the form used by a tenant where there is a dispute following service of Form No. 5 above. It relates to Section 13(4) of the 1988 Housing Act. It can also be used to refer a notice proposing a new rent or licence fee for an assured agricultural occupancy.

ASSURED SHORTHOLD TENANCIES

Assured shorthold tenants can go to the RAC:

a) during the first fixed-term tenancy, without a notice of increase having to be served. This is if the RAC thinks there is a sufficient number of assured lets in the area to allow comparison; and the rent charged is significantly higher than the landlord could expect to get on the basis of these comparisons; or

b) where a notice of increase has been served during a periodic tenancy which has followed a fixed-term tenancy.

For assured shortholds if there is a RAC rent it will become payable on the date set by the RAC (which cannot be earlier than the date of application). If a RAC rent has been set during the first fixed-term tenancy, then and only then is it the maximum payable. The landlord cannot serve another notice of increase until 12 months after the RAC's determination.

It should be noted that the Secretary of State has reserve powers to disapply the assured shorthold rent regulation provisions by area or "other circumstance".

SI 2203 also sets out the form to be used in relation to assured shorthold rents. It is Form No. 8 — Application to a Rent Assessment Committee for a Determination of a Rent Under an Assured Shorthold Tenancy. This is the form used by a tenant with a fixed-term assured shorthold tenancy to apply to the RAC during the fixed-term to have the rent reduced. It can also be used where the fixed-term assured shorthold is an assured agricultural occupancy. It relates to Section 22(1) of the 1988 Housing Act. An application cannot be made if the rent payable under the tenancy is a rent previously determined by a RAC; or it is an assured shorthold tenancy which came into being on the ending of a tenancy which had been an assured shorthold of the same or substantially the same property and the landlord and tenant under each tenancy were the same at that time.

1.6 PREMIUMS (KEY MONEY)

THE ACT ALLOWS LANDLORDS to charge new tenants key money, in other words a sum of money, without limit, simply for the grant of an assured or an assured shorthold tenancy. But note that unless the contrary is agreed, the landlord's consent is not required for assignment or subletting if a premium has been paid.

1.7 SUCCESSION

ALTHOUGH IT IS OPEN to the landlord to give better succession rights, here are the rules under the Act itself.

A. ON THE DEATH OF A RENT ACT STATUTORY TENANT

If an existing Rent Act statutory tenant dies, a surviving spouse (which includes "a person who was living with the original tenant as his or her wife or husband") will have the right to succeed to a protected Rent Act tenancy. (NOTE: there are transitional provisions to protect the successors of tenants who die within 18 months of the Act coming into force).

Other relatives will only have a right to succeed to an assured tenancy — and then only if they have lived with the tenant for the past 2 years (it was 6 months in the Rent Act).

Second successions are only possible if the person who wants to succeed has lived there for the last 2 years and was a member of both the original tenant's family and the first successor's family. Even then, the succession will only be to an assured tenancy.

NOTE: the redevelopment Ground for possession (Ground 6) cannot be used against someone who has become an assured tenant by succession.

B. ON THE DEATH OF AN ASSURED TENANT

If an original assured tenant dies, a surviving spouse (including a person living with the tenant as wife or husband, regardless of marriage) has an automatic right to succeed to an assured tenancy. But relatives will have no right to succeed at all. If such relatives are able to negotiate joint tenancies at the very beginning then they will be in a stronger position if one of them dies. There is no right to a second succession.

C. ON THE DEATH OF AN ASSURED SHORTHOLD TENANT

As an assured shorthold is a type of assured tenancy it would be possible under an assured shorthold periodic tenancy, which came into being after an initial fixed-term, for a spouse to succeed to the tenancy on the death of the tenant.

1.8 RESTRICTED CONTRACT HOLDERS

A. PRE-1988 HOUSING ACT TENANTS

Pre-1988 Housing Act tenants of resident landlords have usually had the status of "restricted contract holders", but the category has also covered some people whose rent covers insubstantial "board" (i.e. food) or substantial "attendances" (e.g. personal services such as cleaning of rooms etc.).

Pre-1988 Housing Act restricted contract holders will keep their present rights (the power of a county court to delay a possession order for up to three months; and the right to apply to a rent tribunal for rent setting). However, the 1988 Housing Act (with effect from January 15th 1989) repeals the power of a local authority to apply to the rent tribunal on a tenant's behalf.

If a restricted contract holder who is the tenant of a resident landlord agrees to a higher or lower rent (and the rent tribunal has not been involved) the tenant will lose restricted contract status, having been assumed to have entered into a new contract under the 1988 Housing Act. The landlord will then be able to serve a notice to quit and get a court possession order, but if the tenant shares accommodation with the landlord s/he will not be covered by the Protection from Eviction Act 1977, and will only be entitled to the notice required by the tenancy — and a court order will not be required (see paragraph 1.10).

The tenant will not be able to go to the rent tribunal, and the court will not have the power to delay a possession order for up to 3 months (its power before the 1988 Act) but will still have the power to delay it for up to 6 weeks in cases of exceptional hardship, or otherwise up to a maximum of 14 days (under section 89 of the 1980 Housing Act).

The question remains — what is the status of the new contract? It cannot be an assured tenancy or an assured shorthold tenancy, because the landlord is resident. There would appear to be two particular situations which might arise:

● The occupant does not share accommodation with the landlord. In this case the occupant will have the basic right from the 1977 Protection from Eviction Act not to be evicted without a court order. A notice to quit will be required. Although the Act itself gives no such label to the status of such an occupant s/he can be called an "unprotected tenant."

● The occupant does share accommodation with the landlord, in which case the landlord will not have to obtain a court order. A notice to quit will be required. It is important to ascertain whether it really is the landlord's only or main home. It will not qualify as such if the landlord only lives there occasionally. Here too the Act is silent as to what these occupants should be called, but the best term is "excluded tenants."

It will continue to be illegal to evict while a tenancy is still in existence, and it can only be ended with a notice. In the case of a periodic tenancy there is a common law right to a Notice to Quit, which in the absence of any agreement to the contrary has, as a minimum requirement, to match the basic period of the tenancy. This is to say that if it is a weekly tenancy there would have to be a minimum 1 week notice; if monthly, a minimum 1 month notice — and so on. To be valid the notice must end no sooner than the last day of a period of the tenancy — for example, if the tenancy runs from Saturday to Friday it would have to end at the earliest on the Friday.

Case law is very old on the question of whether a notice should be in writing. It suggests that it need not be if the tenancy agreement is not in writing, but in view of the nature of the case law in this area landlords would be well advised to give notices in writing.

However, a pre-1988 Housing Act tenant who does not have a resident landlord, will not be affected in this way. If the person is a restricted contract holder (rather than a protected tenant) because a proportion of the rent relates to insubstantial board or substantial attendance; and s/he agrees to pay the landlord a higher or lower rent after January 15th 1989 (and the Rent Tribunal has not been involved) they are in effect agreeing to a new tenancy, and will become assured tenants, unless the landlord can demonstrate that they are licensees rather than tenants. Clearly assured tenants have more rights than restricted contract tenants. This provision could have a significant impact on bed and breakfast lettings. The situation arises because under the

1988 Housing Act the provision of "board" does not prevent a letting from being an assured tenancy. Under the 1977 Rent Act it prevented a letting from being a protected tenancy.

Pre-1988 Housing Act restricted contract holders who have that status because of substantial "attendance" who accept a rent increase after January 15th 1989 could be in a weak position if they were classifiable as licencees rather than tenants.

Schedule 18 of the 1988 Housing Act repeals Section 81A(1)(a) of the 1977 Rent Act. The effect of the change is that an application to cancel a registered rent can be made at any time after registration, instead of having to wait at least 2 years. In consequence of this SI 1988 No. 2195, which came into force on January 15th 1989, amends one of the forms arising from the 1977 Rent Act — the "Application for Cancellation of Rent Registered by a Rent Tribunal." — by removing the words: "At least 2 years have elapsed since the rent was entered on the register."

B. NEW TENANTS

There will be no new "restricted contract" lets. New tenants of resident landlords will have no security of tenure other than a notice to quit and a 28 day court order (except for the section 89 of the 1980 Housing Act court powers mentioned in A. above). They will have to pay whatever rent is demanded by the landlord. In some cases they may not have even the limited protection of the 1977 Protection from Eviction Act (see 1.10 below). Their status will be that of excluded contractual tenants (see also A. above).

The definition of "resident landlord" for new lets is generally the same as under the Rent Act, but a small change enables the trustees of a deceased resident landlord to avoid giving an assured tenancy to an existing tenant in the same accommodation.

A new landlord who moves in, and persuades an assured tenant to move to another part of the house, does not qualify as a resident landlord.

NOTE: If the tenant shares accommodation with the landlord, see 1.10 below.

1.9 HARASSMENT AND ILLEGAL EVICTION

THE ACT INTRODUCES TWO major changes:- an additional, and tougher, harassment offence (while keeping a revised version of the old one); and tougher rules for compensation after unlawful eviction. These changes cover new and existing residential occupiers.

A. AN ADDITIONAL OFFENCE OF HARASSMENT

The Act amends the 1977 Protection from Eviction Act to strengthen its harassment provisions.

a) The Act strengthens the existing remedy against the criminal offence of harassment. An objective test will apply, which is that acts of harassment are **likely** to interfere with the peace and comfort of residential occupiers. This replaces the pre-1988 Act position, where an occupier had to prove that such acts were **calculated** to cause such interference.

b) The Act introduces an **additional** criminal offence of harassment. Under it, as well as what amounts to a repeat of the new objective test already noted, there is another one. The previous position was that there had to be proof that the landlord intended the occupier to give up possession, or refrain from taking up rights. But now, all that has to be proved is that the landlord **"knows, or has reasonable cause to believe"** that the conduct is likely to have that effect.

Landlords can use as a defence "reasonable grounds" for "doing the acts or withdrawing or withholding the services in question."

B. COMPENSATION FOR UNLAWFUL EVICTION

The Act introduces a new right, under the **civil** law, for compensation (civil damages) to be payable where a landlord or landlord's agent (after 9th June 1988) unlawfully deprives (or attempts unlawfully to deprive) a residential occupier of the whole or part of any premises which are occupied; or does acts **likely** to make a person leave or **persistently withdraws** or **withholds** services, **knowing, or having reasonable cause to believe**, that it will make the person leave or not enforce rights, and the person leaves as a result.

In such cases the tenant can ask the county court for **compensation**, which will be calculated on the basis of the difference between the tenanted and vacant possession value of the accommodation.

Valuations will make certain assumptions:
a) sale by the landlord on the open market to a willing buyer;
b) neither the residential occupier nor a family member wants to buy the accommodation; and
c) "substantial" development and demolition is unlawful. The valuation can

take account of development potential if it has planning permission under an existing general development order (defined by section 43(3) of the 1971 Town and Country Planning Act), or will amount to a change of use by the creation of more dwelling-houses via conversion.

In practice the development value taken into consideration will be that relating to the potential conversion of a house into flats, and even if a tenant does go to court they will not necessarily get the amount the landlord actually gains from the eviction. It seems also that the level of security will play a part, so an evicted shorthold tenant will lose out even more. A concern is, with higher levels of compensation available, that the courts will be less ready to order that the evicted person is reinstated in the accommodation.

Cases can be heard in the county court or the High Court.

Landlords have two defences. They can claim that they had "believed, or had reasonable cause to believe" that the occupier had left; or that they had "reasonable grounds" for "doing the acts or withdrawing or withholding the services in question."

Landlords also have two other get-outs:

The first concerns **reinstatement**. The court can decide that there is no liability to pay damages if the former residential occupier is reinstated "before the date on which proceedings to enforce liability are finally disposed of", or where the court orders reinstatement (whether or not by an injunction) at the request of the former residential occupier.

The second concerns conduct, and has three parts. The court can "reduce the amount of damages which would otherwise be payable to such an amount as it thinks appropriate" where:
a) the conduct of the former residential occupier or anyone living with her/him was "such that it is reasonable to mitigate the damages", or
b) before the beginning of proceedings, the landlord had offered reinstatement which had been turned down unreasonably. If the offer of reinstatement is made after the former residential occupier has obtained alternative accommodation then the court has to ignore that fact — i.e. it has to assume that the person is literally homeless.

1.10 EVICTION WITHOUT A COURT ORDER

This is a case of two small steps forward — one giant step backward.

The Act amends section 3 of the 1977 Protection from Eviction Act (court order needed to evict) to include licences as well as tenancies. And it applies section 5 of that Act (4 week written notices to quit) to periodic licences (but not excluded licences — see below). The amendments cover licences granted before 15th January 1989 as well as those granted afterwards.

But at the same time it says a court order will not be needed to evict tenants and licensees in a number of situations. These "exclusions" affect certain licences entered into before January 15th 1989, or subject to contract made before that date. They do not affect licences which arise on or after January 15th 1989. They can only affect tenancies entered into on or after that date. Pre-January 15th 1989 tenancies cannot be excluded. The exclusion categories are as follows:

● Tenants and licensees who share accommodation with the landlord or licensor, which is part of that person's "only or principal home". The Act defines "accommodation" for these purposes as — "neither an area used for storage nor a staircase, passage, corridor or other means of access";

● Tenants and licensees who live in the same building as the landlord or licensor (as long as it is not a purpose built block of flats) and who share accommodation (as above) with a member of that person's family (for definition of family member see section 113, 1985 Housing Act);

● Tenants and licensees with a right to occupy for a holiday;

● People who originally entered that or any other accommodation as trespassers but who were granted a tenancy or a licence as a "temporary expedient";

● A licensee in a local authority, development corporation, Housing Corporation, housing association, HAT, or other public sector hostel. But note that the Act gives the Secretary of State power to extend the exclusions to other hostel landlords.

● Tenants or licensees where no rent is payable. This was put in to cover the situation where, for example, someone is put up on a friend's floor. Although it appears that agricultural tied tenancies and licences may not be excluded under this provision, there is some doubt over non-agricultural arrangements.

These excluded tenants or licensees will only be entitled to whatever notice is required by their contract.

1.11 REPAIRS

See 5.7 and 5.8 below.

1.12 OTHER ISSUES

A. ASSIGNMENT AND SUBLETTING

It is an implied term of every periodic assured tenancy that unless the contract permits or prohibits it, or a premium has been paid, there can be no assignment or sub-letting without the landlord's consent. And in a change from the 1977 Rent Act position, tenants will not be able to claim that consent was unreasonably withheld.

B. WHERE THE LANDLORD IS ALSO A TENANT/OR SUB-LEASES THE TENANCY

If the "immediate" landlord is a tenant of someone else, called a "superior" landlord, and their tenancy comes to an end, the assured tenant becomes an assured tenant of the "superior" landlord (unless the nature of that landlord is such that it is prevented by the Act from granting an assured tenancy).

If the "immediate" landlord has sub-leased to another landlord, the tenant becomes an assured tenant of that landlord.

C. DISTRESS FOR RENT

In order to "levy distress" a landlord has to obtain permission from the county court. The court has the same powers to adjourn proceedings, or to stay, suspend, or postpone any order made, as it has concerning possession actions.

NOTE: "Distress" is sometimes called "distraint". Both terms mean the same thing — the landlord's right to seize a person's goods (some but not all) in order to sell them to cover a debt owed (including rent arrears), as long as certain procedures are followed.

D. AMENDMENTS TO THE 1987 LANDLORD AND TENANT ACT

Leaseholders of flats which include common parts are given the right of first refusal where the landlord wants to sell, and the right to have defects in their leases corrected. Assured tenants are excluded from the right of first refusal.

E. NON-TENANT SPOUSES, RIGHTS ON BREAKDOWN OF RELATIONSHIP

The 1983 Matrimonial Homes Act will be applied to assured tenants and assured agricultural occupants, which means that in certain circumstances non-tenant spouses will have the right to remain in their homes and apply to the court for the tenancy to be transferred after a relationship breakdown.

In the case of a married spouse, under the 1983 Matrimonial Homes Act (as amended by the 1988 Housing Act) the partner who remains occupies as the tenant but does not have the actual status of tenant. This is why, if divorce proceedings are taken, it is very important that the partner remaining in occupation should be advised to apply for a vesting order, to transfer the tenancy to them. If this application is not made, and the divorce settlement does not involve a transfer of the tenancy, the occupant will have no protection on divorce.

In the case of a spouse who is not married there is no statutory mechanism for the transfer of a tenancy following a relationship breakdown, unless some kind of sub-letting arrangement can be made between the tenant and the non-tenant partner. However, this is doubtful unless the sub-tenancy is lawful — i.e. if it is allowed by the tenancy agreement or if the Act's implied term against sub-letting is overturned by the fact that a premium has been paid for the grant of the tenancy.

It may be the case that the landlord offers, and the non-tenant spouse accepts, a new tenancy of the accommodation. If the old tenancy was a statutory or protected tenancy under the 1977 Rent Act then the new tenancy would be an assured tenancy under the 1988 Housing Act. If the remaining partner is a married spouse then if such an offer is made, and the person concerned wants to preserve a higher level of protection than under an assured tenancy they should ensure that in divorce proceedings they apply for an order vesting the statutory or protected tenancy in themself.

F. INFORMATION — LOCAL AUTHORITY POWERS

Under section 149 of the 1977 Rent Act local authorities have powers to publish information "for the benefit of landlords and tenants with respect to their rights and duties under certain enactments". These powers are extended to encompass assured tenancies, assured shorthold tenancies, and assured agricultural occupancies — but not notably, the protection from eviction, phasing out of the Rent Acts, and the general provisions parts of the private rented sector part of the Act. This is a curious omission, and appears to be an oversight.

G. SHARED OWNERSHIP

The rental part of future shared ownership schemes will be subject to the assured tenancy rules.

H. RENT BOOKS

Section 5 of the 1985 Landlord and Tenant Act covers the information which has to be contained in rent books. The 1988 Housing Act applies these rules to assured tenancies. SI 1988 No. 2198, which came into force on January 15th 1989, amends the 1982 Rent Book (Forms of Notice) Regulations by adding a form of notice which is to be included in rent books or other similar documents, where the accommodation is subject to an assured tenancy, an assured shorthold tenancy, or an assured agricultural occupancy.

I. NOTICES TO QUIT

As already mentioned in 1.4, notices to quit cannot be used under the assured or assured shorthold regime. Notices Seeking Possession (NOSPs) are used instead. However, they will still be useable in other circumstances. SI 1988 No. 2201, which came into force on January 15th 1989, sets out the information which has to be included in a notice to quit given after that date. If it is not included the notice to quit will be invalid and a court order should not be granted if a county court is later asked to grant a possession order.

The information is as follows:

1. If the tenant or licensee does not leave the dwelling, the landlord or licensor must get an order for possession from the court before they can lawfully be evicted. The landlord or licensor cannot apply for such an order before the notice to quit or notice to determine has run out;
2. A tenant or licensee who does not know if s/he has any right to remain in possession after a notice to quit or a notice to determine runs out, can obtain advice from a solicitor. Help with all or part of the cost of legal advice and assistance may be available under the Legal Aid Scheme. S/he should also be able to obtain information from a Citizens' Advice Bureau, a Housing Aid Centre or a rent officer.

J. LICENCE/TENANCY — NON EXCLUSIVE OCCUPATION LICENCES

Towards the end of 1988 the House of Lords came to a judgment on two cases — see below. These were the first to be decided by the Lords on this issue since Street v Mountford (1985), when Lord Templeman set out three determinants for a tenancy — exclusive occupation (based in fact, not in what is written in an agreement); letting for a term (i.e. periodic or fixed-term); and that rent is payable.

As a result of the judgments in these latest cases there is now a limited scope for non-exclusive occupation licence agreements as a means of avoiding statutory protection:

After Antoniades v Villiers
They will not work where 2 or more people apply jointly to rent accommodation, where in fact (not what is written on the agreement) they are given exclusive occupation, and where rent is payable. In such a case it will be a joint tenancy. A landlord's claim to have the right to share the accommodation will be meaningless, and a pretence. The courts will look also at whether the landlord has actually done anything to bring anyone in after the agreement has been made.

After AG Securities v Vaughan
They may work successfully where a shifting group of individuals agree to share with people who are initially strangers and where there is a shifting use of individual parts of the premises — such as bedrooms. Where there is not such a shifting use people may still be able to claim that they have exclusive use of their own parts (e.g. bedrooms).

It is inevitable that there will be more litigation on the points raised here, with other cases being decided in the Court of Appeal and by the Law Lords.

1.13 ASSURED AGRICULTURAL OCCUPANCIES

A. THE CONCEPT
The Act creates the concept of "assured agricultural occupancies" for tenancies and licences created after January 15th 1989 — for agricultural workers who meet an "agricultural worker condition". The Act says that all such "occupancies" are to be treated as assured tenancies. The list of tenancies which cannot be assured tenancies applies (see the list in Schedule 1 of the Act), except for nos. 3 (no rent, or the rent is less than two-thirds of the rateable value) and 7 (tenancies of agricultural holdings). Licencees must also have exclusive occupation and "sufficient interest" in

the accommodation. There is also a "qualifying ownership" test for landlord/employers.

A "qualifying worker" is defined in Schedule 3 of this Act and of the 1976 Rent (Agriculture) Act as someone who has worked in agriculture for 91 out of the last 104 weeks, or who is incapable of work due to injury or disease.

B. SUCCESSION

A spouse or cohabitee can succeed to an assured agricultural occupancy, as can a family member who has lived with the occupant for 2 years prior to the death.

C. SECURITY OF TENURE

If the tenant gives the employer notice to terminate employment it does not constitute a notice to quit the occupancy.

The assured tenure Grounds for possession can be used, with the exception of Ground 16 (the letting was in consequence of employment, and the tenant has ceased to be in that employment).

SI 1988 No. 2203 sets out the prescribed form concerning notice seeking possession. It is Form No. 4 — Notice Seeking Possession of an Assured Agricultural Occupancy. This notice can be used by the landlord (or licensor). It relates to Section 8 of the 1988 Housing Act.

The provision under the 1976 Rent (Agriculture) Act is extended to include assured agricultural occupancies. This applies where the accommodation is needed for another worker, the employer does not have a suitable alternative, and it is in the interests of efficient agriculture, and in the circumstances local authorities have to use their "best endeavours" to rehouse agricultural workers.

2. Housing Associations

INTRODUCTION

Housing associations run a housing stock of over 500,000 homes. They are non-profit making bodies regulated in England by the Housing Corporation, a government agency, (in Wales, by Housing for Wales (Tai Cymru); in Scotland by Scottish Homes.) Their central aim is to provide good quality, secure rented homes for people on low incomes. The vast bulk of this provision is financed from public funds.

The Housing Act and other government proposals have brought profound changes to the housing association movement. The proportion of public funding has been considerably reduced, forcing an increasing reliance on private funding; and associations now have to share the private rented sector security of tenure and rents regime. As a result the movement has been plunged into a serious identity crisis, as it ponders whether it can survive as a provider of affordable housing for people on low incomes — or whether it will be pushed up-market.

Although the Act itself does not set the new funding balance (changes do not need legislation), funding dominated the debate during passage of the Bill — for all the other issues depend on it. When the Bill was published the Government was proposing that instead of nearly all the funding being public money, future schemes should be based on a 30% public / 70% private split. Then Ministers decided to opt for a 50% public / 50% split. They then proposed a 50% to 75% average for public funding. As explained below, just before Christmas 1988 the final arrangement was announced — a 75% public funding average, with no upper limit.

New lets from January 15th 1989 are assured or assured shorthold tenancies (the latter is theoretically allowed by the Act).

Many of the rules concerning security of tenure, rents, and other tenancy terms, are similar to those which the Act applies to the private rented sector. We deal with these first, and then go on to cover Part II of the Act, which deals with the structure and function of housing associations; and relevant provisions — e.g. concerning repairs, and anti-racism, arising from later parts of the Act.

The Government was able to bring about a fundamental change to "mixed funding" for housing associations without legislation, so the Act makes no mention of it. On December 14th 1988 the Government announced the balance of funding — the public contribution would be reduced to an average of 75% of total funding in 1989 (for England, Wales and Scotland) the rest being made up from private funding. There will be no upper limit for the public funding element. The Housing Corporation made a later announcement on the regional proportions.

2.1 A NEW FORM OF TENANCY FOR NEW LETS

IN GENERAL, AS REGARDS SECURITY of tenure and rents, the rules applied by the Housing Act 1988 to private renting will apply to housing association letting. From January 15th 1989 associations have had to let on the basis of "assured" tenancies. Although the Act itself allows housing associations to use "assured shorthold" tenancies, the Housing Corporation has issued guidance advising them not to in general. The guidance does not amount to an absolute ban. All will depend on interpretation.

Associations will not normally be able to let on the basis of the pre-Housing Act 1988 protection (security:- secure tenancy under the Housing Act 1985, rent:- subject to the Rent Act 1977). There are a few exceptions

a) the contract was entered into before January 15th 1989;
b) immediately beforehand the tenant was a housing association tenant of the same housing association (see 2.3 for details);
c) it is ordered as such by a county court as suitable alternative accommodation; or
d) where a housing association buys a property with a sitting protected tenant.

At the end of 1988 the Housing Corporation published a document called — "Tenants' Guarantee: Guidance on the Management by Registered Housing Associations of Housing Accommodation let on ASSURED TENANCIES under the Housing Act 1988". It was introduced by Housing Corporation Circular 8c.43/88. It covers all new tenants of registered housing associations after January 15th 1989. This document, and the National Federation of Housing Association's Model Tenancy Agreement which is attached to it, re-introduces as contractual rights many of the 1985 Housing Act "Tenants' Charter" rights. However, the Grounds for possession are different, as they are those contained in the 1988 Housing Act, not those in the 1985 Housing Act. The document recommends that only six of the 1988 Act Grounds should be used by housing associations — Grounds 7, 9, 10, 12, 13 and 14. Note also that new tenants will not have the Right to Buy, or the right to apply for a portable discount.

The NFHA has also produced a model assured tenancy agreement for special needs shared housing, and a model licence for residents of shared housing.

It is important to note that neither the "Tenants' Guarantee" nor the Model Tenancy Agreement has statutory force. If any dispute arises over the level of rights a court of law would base its judgment on the 1988 Housing Act itself, not these documents, although if a tenant sought court redress before the landlord took court action (contrary to the contract) to utilise a provision under the Act (e.g. a possession ground) they might be able to persuade the court to issue an injunction against the landlord.

2.2 PRE-JANUARY 15th 1989 HOUSING ASSOCIATION TENANTS STILL PROTECTED BY THE RENT ACT 1977 AND THE HOUSING ACT 1985

TENANTS ALREADY PROTECTED by the Rent Act 1977 (a housing association tenancy as concerns rents), and the Housing Act 1985 (the security of tenure part of the Tenants' Charter), will keep that protection during that tenancy but suffer a reduction of rights aimed specifically at existing housing association tenants. The Act (paragraph 24, Schedule 17) has abolished the two year phasing in of rent officer fair rents for the housing association sector. This brings it into line with the private rented sector. Rent registration will still take place every two years, but any increased rent will be payable straight away. It affects all cases where the registration date of the fair rent was on or after January 15th 1989 — (SI 1988 No. 2152). If the registration date was before January 15th 1989 but the effective date was on or after that date phasing will still apply for that registration.

2.3 PRE-JANUARY 15th 1989 HOUSING ASSOCIATION TENANTS RIGHTS FOLLOWING A MOVE

AFTER JANUARY 15TH 1989, if an existing tenant (already protected by the Rent Act 1977 and the Housing Act 1985), is offered alternative accommodation by their present housing association — either in the same house, or in another house the association owns — the tenant will keep the existing protection.

In addition, existing tenants will keep their right to a mutual exchange by way of assignment. This means that a tenant can exchange homes with another secure tenant, including where the other person is a local authority tenant. In effect the tenants swap, but the actual tenancies do not end — having been assigned. If a secure tenant wants to swap with an assured housing association tenant there is a contractual right (but not a statutory right) to do so. In any case where a housing association landlord initiates a transfer of a new or existing tenant, after the transfer the tenant will be a secure tenant if it is the same housing association; and an assured tenant if the transfer has been to a different housing association.

2.4 TENANTS WHOSE ACCOMMODATION IS TAKEN OVER BY A HOUSING ASSOCIATION

IF HOUSING ASSOCIATIONS TAKE over private rented accommodation, with protected or statutory sitting tenants under the Rent Act, those tenants will become secure tenants under the Housing Act 1985 (as concerns security of tenure) and housing association tenants (as concerns rent registration) under the Rent Act 1977, not assured tenants.

If housing associations take over accommodation (e.g. under the "change of landlord" proposals, or voluntary transfer of council housing) with sitting secure tenants, those tenants will become assured tenants, with the Right to Buy preserved.

If housing associations take over other housing association property the tenants will remain protected by the Housing Act 1985 for security of tenure, and by the Rent Act 1977 for rent registration.

2.5 ASSURED TENANCY SECURITY

ASSURED TENANCIES CAN BE periodic (such as weekly or monthly), or fixed-term (the Act does not specify a minimum or maximum term). It is unlikely that housing associations will use fixed-term tenancies.

To evict a periodic tenant a housing association will first have to give the tenant a written Notice Seeking Possession (NOSP) which will have to say why it wants the tenant to leave, and what specific 1988 Housing Act Ground for possession it wants to use. The Grounds are the same as those available to private landlords (but see 2.1 above on the Housing Corporation's recommendations that only certain Grounds should be used). The NOSP will be 2 weeks or 2 months depending on the Ground used. When the NOSP expires the association has up to 12 months to ask the county court to make a possession order. In the case of some Grounds for possession the court has discretion to refuse a possession order — that is to say the tenant has a defence, even if the Ground is proved.

To evict the tenant when a fixed term assured tenancy comes to an end (or during it if the association alleges that the tenant has breached the contract, and if the agreement allows termination for breach) it has to serve a NOSP and satisfy the court that there is a Ground for possession.

2.6 ASSURED TENANCY RENTS

NEW HOUSING ASSOCIATION SCHEMES will be financed by an average of 75% Housing Association Grant (HAG), with the rest coming from the private sector. This is in place of the previous system based on a Government grant of nearly 100%. There will however be no upper limit for the public funding element.

Rents will be set by the housing association. Tenants will not be able to go to the Rent Officer to register a 'fair rent'. Instead, the Rent Assessment Committee (RAC) will take on the rent registration role. But tenants will not have a right to go to the RAC during the first year of the tenancy to challenge the rent charged.

Where a rent is registered by the RAC it will be at what the RAC considers the market rent. Even if the RAC registers a rent the Act allows housing association landlords to seek their tenants' agreement to a higher rent. The Housing Corporation's Tenants' Guarantee rules say that rents charged by housing associations will generally be below market rents. If so, it is difficult to see how the RAC can be the right body to act as an arbiter on rents.

2.7 KEY MONEY (PREMIUMS)

THE ACT DOES NOT PROHIBIT housing associations charging new tenants key money, in other words a sum of money, without limit, simply for the grant of a tenancy. Until this Act it had been assumed that associations could not make such charges. However, the Housing Corporation's "Tenants' Guarantee" makes it clear that action will be taken against associations which do attempt to make such charges.

2.8 SUCCESSION

ALTHOUGH IT IS OPEN to the landlord to give better succession rights here are the rules under the Act itself.

A. ON THE DEATH OF A PRE-HOUSING ACT 1988 TENANT

If a pre-Housing Act 1988 secure tenant dies, surviving spouses (or another relative if there is no surviving spouse) will keep the right to succeed to a secure tenancy under the 1985 Housing Act. But note — this still means only one succession, and in the case of a non-spouse relative that person will have to have lived in the tenant's home for the last year of the tenant's life.

B. ON THE DEATH OF AN ASSURED TENANT

Under the Act if an assured tenant dies, surviving spouses and cohabitees have an automatic right to succeed to an assured tenancy. But relatives will have no right to succeed at all. However, the Model Tenancy Agreement reproduces as a contractual right the statutory succession rights of secure tenants under the 1985 Housing Act. As was the case before the 1988 Act there is no right to a second succession.

Note however that these rights should not be confused with the succession rights of tenants who have opted to remain with a local authority landlord under the "tenants' choice" proposal — see 4. below.

2.9 HARASSMENT AND ILLEGAL EVICTION

THE PROVISIONS OUTLINED in 1.9 above will apply to housing associations as well as to private landlords.

It should also be noted that the Model Tenancy Agreement contains the following recommendation concerning use of possession Ground 14 (nuisance):

"The tenant or anyone living in the premises has caused persistent nuisance or annoyance to neighbours or has been responsible for any act of harassment on the Grounds of race, colour, sex or disability, or has been convicted of using the premises for immoral or illegal purposes."

2.10 EVICTION WITHOUT A COURT ORDER

THE PROVISIONS OUTLINED in 1.10 above will apply to housing associations as well as to private landlords. The key issue for associations will be the development of policy and practice regarding licensees in housing association hostels.

2.11 MUTUAL EXCHANGES

THERE ARE FIVE circumstances to consider:

1. Two pre-January 15th 1989 housing association secure tenants exchange. In this case the 1988 Housing Act changes nothing. Each will remain a secure tenant under the Housing Act 1985 as concerns security of tenure; and a housing association tenant under the Rent Act 1977 as concerns rent (i.e. the Rent Officer sets and registers a "fair" rent).

2. A pre-January 15th 1989 housing association secure tenant exchanges with a post-January 15th 1989 housing association assured tenant. In this case both will become assured tenants under the 1988 Housing Act.

3. A post-January 15th 1989 housing association assured tenant exchanges with a post-January 15th 1989 housing association assured tenant. In this case both will become assured tenants under the 1988 Housing Act, but the housing association will not be able to increase the rent at this point.

4. A local authority secure tenant exchanges with a pre-January 15th 1989 housing association secure tenant. In this case the person taking over the council tenancy takes on that secure tenancy (i.e. secure under the 1985 Housing Act), and the person taking over the housing association tenancy becomes a secure tenant under the 1985 Housing Act as concerns security of tenure; and a housing association tenant under the Rent Act 1977 as concerns rent (i.e. the Rent Officer sets and registers a "fair" rent).

5. A council secure tenant exchanges with a post-January 15th 1989 housing association assured tenant. In this case the person who has been the council tenant takes over the housing association assured tenancy by way of

assignment; and the person who has been the housing association tenant, rather than taking over the existing council tenancy, is granted a new council tenancy.

NOTE: Section 91 of the Housing Act 1985 says that a secure tenant can only assign to another secure tenant.

Structural and functional changes for housing associations

These are set out in Part II of the Act. Unless other dates are given in the text they were brought into force on April 1st 1989 by SI 1989 No. 404. (With the exception of the relation of Section 59 to paragraph 27 of Schedule 6). Note that SI 1989 No. 404 also contains detailed provisos relating to repeal and amendment of legislation affecting a number of issues which are dealt with in this part of the Guide. These are referred to later in the Guide, at 5.12 — CONSEQUENTIAL ISSUES.

2.12 WALES AND SCOTLAND

THE HOUSING CORPORATION WILL continue to act as the governing body for housing associations in England. In Wales a new body — Housing for Wales — will have a similar function. The Housing (Scotland) Act 1988 has set up a similar body for Scotland — Scottish Homes.

Parts of the Act relating to Housing for Wales and Scottish Homes came into force on December 1st 1988. These are Sections 46(1) and (2); 47(2); part of 47(6); and the relevant part of 140(1).

Housing for Wales will have between 6 and 8 board members. The Secretary of State for Wales appoints them and the Chief Executive can dismiss them, decide how board meetings are to be run, board remuneration, and how many staff there should be.

2.13 WIDER FUNCTIONS FOR HOUSING ASSOCIATIONS

These include:

a) providing land, amenities, and services; and providing, constructing, repairing or improving buildings, to benefit their residents. They can do this alone or with other bodies.

b) acquiring, repairing, improving, or converting properties for sale — on a lease or share-ownership basis.

c) building for sale on a shared ownership basis.

d) managing houses or blocks of flats on leasehold which are owned by individuals or non-housing association organisations.

e) setting up agency services to carry out, arrange or encourage maintenance, repair or improvement. The housing association movement has received Government confirmation that these services can go beyond housing services. For example, they can include care as well as repair schemes for elderly owner-occupiers.

f) encouraging and advising on setting up, servicing or running other housing associations and voluntary housing organisations.

g) acquiring (and repairing, improving or converting) commercial premises or businesses incidental to the associations' work; and for a limited period to carry on any business acquired.

h) repairing or improving houses or buildings containing houses, after tenants have set in motion or exercised the Right to Buy.

i) acquiring houses to be sold at a discount (under the portable discount scheme) to tenants of Charitable housing associations — who cannot exercise the Right to Buy.

2.14 HOUSING CORPORATION MANAGEMENT GUIDANCE TO ASSOCIATIONS

THE ISSUE OF MANAGEMENT guidance by the Housing Corporation is governed by Section 49 of the 1988 Housing Act, and this section came into force on January 15th 1989.

Such guidance can be issued and enforced by the Corporation, and can vary according to the type of association, the type of accommodation, and the area. It "may" cover housing needs which are to be met, and how;

allocations; tenancy terms and rent setting; maintenance and repair standards; and consultation and communication with tenants. But it should be remembered that such guidance will not have legislative force. The courts would be bound to enforce the statute, not the guidance.

The Housing Corporation has to submit its proposed guidance to consultation with bodies representative of housing associations, and the Secretary of State's approval is needed. The National Federation of Housing Associations has produced a recommended Model Tenancy Agreement, which, as already stated, has received Housing Corporation approval and has been attached to the "Tenants' Guarantee". We also cover the latter in the section of this Guide on the Act's "Change of Landlord" provisions.

2.15 GRANTS

The Housing Corporation is given wide powers to determine grant levels and procedures, subject to approval by the Secretary of State. General determinations will depend on Treasury consent. But before making a general determination the Corporation has to consult "bodies appearing to be representative of housing associations".

Under Section 57 (which came into force on January 15th 1989) the Act gives the Secretary of State power to delegate functions to the Housing Corporation (including tax relief grants; the rent surplus fund; and functions which remain under the Housing Associations Act 1985).

Although it is not stated in the Act itself, there is a Government commitment that "full public funding" will be available for "certain kinds of schemes, and also certain associations which for a variety of reasons will find it difficult to attract mixed-funding." This means that some associations will be able to fund through public loans (i.e. Housing Corporation or local authority mortgage) not through private loans, what they cannot get through HAG.

A. HOUSING ASSOCIATION GRANTS (HAG)

Before the Act the Secretary of State had the grant-making powers but delegated them to the Corporation and to local authorities to act as agents for the payment of the grant. Under the Act the Corporation alone has the power to make grants to registered housing associations concerning spending on housing activities (on the basis of the much wider definition already outlined). The Corporation decides the application procedure; the circumstances in which grant is payable; how it is calculated; how and when it is paid; and the conditions attached to it.

The Housing Corporation will still be able to appoint local authorities as agents in the payment of grant, although the consent of both the Secretary of State and the Treasury will be needed. This may well mean that the pre-Act bureaucracy of "double scrutiny" (whereby schemes were vetted by the Department of the Environment as well as the local authority) may still be a feature of the new arrangement.

HAG paid via a local authority will not be cash limited. The same rules will apply as apply to other schemes. The full cost of the scheme will count against the local authority's Housing Investment Programme (HIP).

Local authority schemes for the promotion and funding of projects which satisfy HAG rules will automatically attract HAG, payable by the Corporation.

B. REVENUE DEFICIT GRANT

This grant was paid before the 1988 Housing Act to cover deficits. There was also a Hostel Deficit Grant. The Act abolishes the latter. But the Housing Corporation will still be able to pay the Hostel Deficit Grant if an association is in deficit on its hostel activities, as for the the purposes of this grant the Act gives the Corporation power to consider all or only part of an association's activities.

In operating these powers the Corporation can lay down and change rules and act on assumptions concerning for example — rents. The Government has indicated that special needs activities in general will be given separate consideration.

The Government would like to phase out this grant.

C. RECOVERY OF GRANTS

The Corporation (previously the Secretary of State) can reduce, suspend or cancel payment of grant; order the association to pay some or all of it back; or (a new power) order the payment of interest.

D. TAX RELIEF GRANTS

The Act reproduces the Secretary of State's existing power to make grants by way of tax relief (for income tax and corporation tax) to most non-charitable associations. It also makes the position clear that the measure covers shared ownership housing.

E. RENT SURPLUS FUND

The pre-Act position was that associations had to set up a "Grant Redemption Fund", to enable any rental surplus arising out of HAG-funded development, repair or improvement of properties, to be repaid to central government.

The Act repeals these provisions. In their place, where grant-aided registered housing associations have surpluses from rents they will have to note them in their accounts as a rent surplus fund. The Secretary of State has wide powers in deciding how surpluses are to be calculated — and again, rent levels will be an important element in his assumptions. He will consult on these decisions.

The Secretary of State can order the repayment of any surplus, with interest; and he can make associations provide relevant information.

Although not stated in the Act itself, the Government has given indications that a very substantial part of the Rent Surplus Fund may be kept by housing associations for future major repairs, and for reserves. Reserves will be very important for associations, who will wish to continue letting to the same categories of tenants, while at the same time having to work with a higher risk strategy and satisfy investors that they are financially safe. The central issue here concerns Government intentions concerning the extent to which the surpluses are "clawed-back" into central government funds.

SI 1989 No. 327, which came into force on April 1st 1989, makes consequential amendments to the Registered Housing Associations (Accounting Requirements) Order 1988. Apart from substituting "Rent Surplus Fund" for "Grant Redemption Fund", the SI also omits references to the Grant Redemption Fund in relation to co-ownership societies and almshouses, as they will not have to maintain Rent Surplus Funds.

2.16 ANTI-RACISM

UNDER SECTION 71 OF THE RACE RELATIONS ACT 1976 the Housing Corporation, Housing for Wales, (and Scottish Homes under the Housing (Scotland) Act 1988) have a duty to eliminate racial discrimination and promote equal opportunities.

But the duty will not apply to individual housing associations, except through these bodies.

The NFHA has produced its own guidelines — "Race and Housing" and urges individual housing associations to adopt key practices where they are operating in areas where the black and other ethnic minority communities exceed 2% of the population. These include keeping ethnic records and monitoring for allocations and employment; fair access; the establishment of links with ethnic minority communities; management committees are to reflect the ethnic make-up of the area; and a clear policy on racial harassment.

2.17 PORTABLE DISCOUNT SCHEMES

UNDER THE HOUSING ASSOCIATIONS ACT 1985 charitable housing associations could run portable discount schemes. Under HOTCHA (The Home Ownership scheme for the Tenants of Charitable Housing Associations) such associations can buy dwellings on the market and resell them on Right to Buy terms to their tenants or licencees. Funds are limited, and payment is discretionary. The scheme was set up to compensate for the fact that tenants of charitable associations do not have the Right to Buy. The Housing Act 1988 re-enacts the scheme, and includes property owned by such an association where there has been a HAG under the new Act.

2.18 OTHER ISSUES

A. PAYMENTS OR BENEFITS

The rules have been relaxed concerning the exemption of certain categories of "payments or benefits" to housing association committee members, officers and employees. The NFHA argued during the passage of the Act that the existing rules had created particular difficulties for relatives of people employed by national associations. This change is aimed at anomalies in previous legislation — e.g. someone could be employed in London by a national housing association, and a close relative living in another part of the country would be barred from being allocated a tenancy by that association.

B. HOUSING CORPORATION POWERS OF INQUIRY CONCERNING MISMANAGEMENT ETC.

The pre-Act powers are widened. Instead of being tied to present or former officers, agents, or members of a housing association, the Corporation will be able to get information from any other body or person it has reason to believe may have relevant information.

2.19 REPAIRS

See 5.7 and 5.8 below.

2.20 CHARITABLE HOUSING ASSOCIATIONS' ACQUISITION OF TENANTED HOUSING FROM PUBLIC AUTHORITIES UNDER "TENANTS' CHOICE" OR VOLUNTARY TRANSFERS

ON APRIL 19TH 1989 HOUSING MINISTER LORD CAITHNESS announced publication of guidance for charitable housing associations considering the acquisition of tenanted housing from public authorities. The guidance, agreed between the Department of the Environment and the Housing Corporation, in consultation with the Charity Commissioners, covers "Tenants' Choice", voluntary transfers, and the winding-up of New Towns. (It can be read in full in Commons Hansard April 19th 1989, col. 229 foll.)

The guidance says that a charitable housing association should only buy tenanted housing if it is — ". . . satisfied that the acquisition will enable it to further its charitable objects and where the acquisition is capable of being regarded objectively in this way." The guidance suggests that this would be achieved if the aim was — ". . . to provide a better service for the existing tenants . . .", and to increase the association's ability — ". . . to provide, in the long term for beneficiaries of the kinds specified in its objects as vacancies arise in the acquired stock." This means tenants who are needy or elderly. But the association could also go ahead with an acquisition even if one of these objectives were not certain — as long as the other was given correspondingly greater weight, and even if the long term aim was to acquire it as an investment for the purposes of providing — ". . . vacant possession gradually over a long period."

After elaborating on these points the guidance goes on to say that transferred tenants' preserved Right to Buy, and other statutory rights — ". . . does not of itself make the purchase inconsistent with the association's charitable objects."

Apart from whether the acquisition fits in with the association's objects, the association will have to consider the proportion of tenants benefiting from the transfer; the extent to which the number of non-beneficiaries will adversely affect management and cause disadvantage to the beneficiaries;

and the expected turnover of non-beneficiaries.

If associations are in doubt they are expected to seek advice from lawyers or from the Charity Commissioners. The NFHA has said it will be prepared to respond to associations' written consultation on these issues.

3. Housing Action Trusts (HATs)

INTRODUCTION

The proposed introduction of Housing Action Trusts has given rise to considerable opposition, especially from the tenants of the areas concerned. Despite a grudging last-minute acceptance by the Government that there should be a ballot of tenants affected, the fact remains that the proposal for a HAT will be a proposal to impose an unelected and unaccountable landlord in the place of the local authority. The initial list of proposed HATs shows that the Government is not even adhering to its original argument that HATs would be set up to take over the worst housing.

The legislation to set up HATs leaves far too many questions unanswered. The fears of tenants, that local people will be forced out by high rents, to be replaced by yuppies; that empty homes will not go to local people; that local labour will not get a look in concerning renovations — all remain unanswered.

Against a backdrop of ministerial drubbings at public meetings, and a series of consultants' reports, the Government has had some second thoughts about its initial list of proposed HATs, but the scheme remains intact, and ballots are awaited.

PART III of the Act, which came into force on November 15th 1988, sets out the framework for the setting up of HATs. HATs themselves will not exist until they have been designated by the Secretary of State, which is subject to a vote of the tenants affected. At the time of writing no votes have been held and consequently there have been no designations. However, the Government has proposed a number of HATs.

The terms of the transfer of housing from local authorities to HATs will be determined by the Secretary of State. It will probably be tenanted market value, but the terms could involve payments to the HAT by the local authority.

3.1 WHAT ARE HATS?

HATs ARE NON-ELECTED BODIES set up by the Government to take over and become the new landlord of a portion of local authority housing (e.g. an estate) and land, and then improve the housing and the environment. The Government plan is for HATs to do this in about 5 years, then wind-up and pass the housing on to someone else.

Six prospective HATs were announced before the Bill became law. The Government plan was that they should include a total of eighteen council estates — over 25,000 homes. The Government's Autumn Statement 1988/89 set aside £192 million for HAT renovation schemes over the three years 1989-90 to 1991-92. The money to enable HATs to buy the housing from the local authorities is separate.

On March 16th 1989 the Secretary of State, Nicholas Ridley, announced that these plans had been revised in the light of consultants' reports. Instead of the original list of 18 estates only 9 will now be included in HATs, in 5 areas instead of the original 6 areas.

Peat Marwick McLintock, and the Property Investment Company Ltd. looked at Lambeth, Tower Hamlets, Southwark, and Sunderland. PIEDA Ltd. "led a consortium" in looking at Leeds. Price Waterhouse "managed" a study in Sandwell.

The consultants estimated renovation costs as — Southwark £112 million; Lambeth between £93 million and £132 million; Sunderland £75 million; Leeds £135 million (on the estates originally proposed); Sandwell £13.5 — £22.4 million on the now dropped Whiteheath estates. There appear to be no DoE plans to enable the £231 million to be spent that the consultants estimated needs to be spent to renovate the six dropped Tower Hamlets estates.

The revised list of proposed HATs is set out below.

Reasons given for the changes varied. The Lambeth, Southwark and Sunderland go-aheads were based on the consultants' conclusions that on the basis of Government criteria (Section 60 of the 1988 Housing Act) HAT designations were justified in these areas. However, in Leeds, although the consultants had concluded that all three of the estates designated originally met the criteria, the Secretary of State had concluded that only Gipton should be designated — as "the most compelling case for a Trust". The decision on Sandwell had been reached on the basis of the strength of the case.

The consultants looking at the Tower Hamlets estates had concluded that the designation of a HAT was justified in the case of all six estates. However, in abandoning the idea of a HAT for any of them Nicholas Ridley cited "overcrowding" which "a Trust could only tackle . . . if it had enough land to provide more housing for the people who now live there. This could involve considerable disruption of the existing communities and would require a much larger area for a Trust than we originally proposed." He also said — "If, after discussion with tenants, the Council wish to bring forward a proposal for a different Trust area, I would be prepared to consider it."

3.2 HATS PROPOSED

Local authorities	Estates
Tower Hamlets	* All plans for a HAT were dropped for all of the estates originally announced — Solander Gardens, Shadwell Gardens, Berner, Boundary, Holland, and part of Ocean.
Leeds	* Gipton (go ahead still planned) * Plans for a HAT were dropped for both Halton Moor and Seacroft South.
Sandwell	* Windmill Lane (go ahead still planned) * A "wider part" of the Cape Hill area next to Windmill Lane (new). The Government asked consultants Price Waterhouse to carry out a further study on whether a HAT should be proceeded with here, and where the boundaries should be. * Whiteheath (the Lion Farm, Wallace Close and Titford estates) — plans for a HAT were dropped.
Lambeth	* Loughborough and Angell Town (go ahead still planned, but with "minor" boundary changes).
Southwark	* North Peckham and Gloucester Grove (go ahead still planned, but with "minor" boundary changes).
Sunderland	* Downhill, Town End Farm, Hylton Castle and part of the Red House estate (go ahead still planned, but with "minor" boundary changes).

3.3 HOW HATS ARE CREATED

THE SECRETARY OF STATE proposes an area to be covered by a HAT. Then either he, or an independent teller, organises a vote of the council tenants eligible to vote. Unless more than half of those who vote are against, the Secretary of

State can designate that area as a HAT, by his power to issue an Order under this Act. If more than half of those who vote are against, the area can not be designated as a HAT.

3.4 WHO CONTROLS HATS?

HATS WILL BE RUN BY A BOARD, with between 7 and 13 members (including the Chair and Vice-Chair), appointed by the Secretary of State for the Environment. There will be some local representation, not necessarily tenants. The Board's meetings have to be open to the public, except for confidential business (just like local authority committees). Agendas and minutes will be available for inspection. Although meetings will be open it should be noted that unlike local authority committees HATs are not subject to the Local Government (Access to Information Act) 1985, which also gives the right to see background papers.

3.5 TENANTS' SECURITY AFTER TRANSFER TO A HAT

HAT TENANTS WILL BE secure tenants, and will therefore keep the security of tenure they had as council tenants under the 1985 Housing Act, including the full Tenants' Charter rights, and the Right to Buy. They will lose certain rights to veto changes proposed by their landlord in the delegation of management and a change of landlord.

3.6 TENANTS' RENTS AFTER TRANSFER TO A HAT

THE DEPARTMENT OF THE ENVIRONMENT has said that rents will be frozen, and then, after improvements, will rise in line with local authority rents, not necessarily related to the cost of improvement.

3.7 TRANSFER TO A NEW LANDLORD DURING THE LIFE OF A HAT

DURING ITS LIFETIME A HAT can pass homes on to new landlords as long as the new landlord is approved by the Housing Corporation (see the "Tenants' Choice" procedure), or to a local authority; if the Secretary of State consents to the transfer. Following a transfer tenants become assured tenants under the Housing Act 1988, and lose their Housing Act 1985 secure tenancy status.

On dissolution of a HAT, during the winding-up process the HAT must try to transfer its homes to an approved body or to a local authority, but ultimately the Secretary of State has the power to transfer remaining homes to any body.

3.8 MOVING IN TO A VACANT HOME DURING THE LIFE OF A HAT

TENANTS COMING IN from outside, or tenants moving from one home to another within a HAT, will become secure tenants. Under Schedule 1 of the 1988 Housing Act a HAT tenant cannot be an assured tenant.

3.9 WHAT HAPPENS AT THE END OF A HAT

WHEN IMPROVEMENTS HAVE BEEN completed the HAT has to wind-up, and dispose of its housing. This will probably mean sale to other landlords. HAT tenants have a right to have their homes taken back by the council only if the council wants to do so — in other words if it can afford to buy the homes. The new landlord can be anybody — a private landlord, a housing association, the council, or a co-operative — as long as they are approved by the Housing Corporation under the "Tenants' Choice" procedure. Tenants will not have a veto over who their new landlord will be. Unless the council buys the property back the tenants will become assured tenants under the 1988 Housing Act, and lose their Housing Act 1985 secure tenancy status.

3.10 ANTI-RACISM

UNDER SECTION 71 OF THE 1976 RACE RELATIONS ACT HATs have a duty to eliminate racial discrimination and promote equal opportunities.

3.11 HOMELESSNESS

EVEN THOUGH THEY WILL be made up of large sections of taken-over council housing HATs will have no duty to house homeless people. They are expected to co-operate (under the weak Section 72 of the Housing Act 1985) to help local authorities carry out their homelessness duties.

3.12 CHRONICALLY SICK AND DISABLED PEOPLE

HATS WILL HAVE TO HAVE REGARD to the needs of chronically sick and disabled people (section 3 of the 1970 Chronically Sick and Disabled Persons Act will apply to HATs — by Order). And disability will not be a ground for dismissal from the Board of a HAT (or from the Housing Corporation or Housing for Wales).

Local authorities' views will have to be taken into account as to whether homes specially provided for elderly and disabled people should be transferred to a HAT.

3.13 OTHER POWERS TRANSFERRED FROM LOCAL AUTHORITIES TO HATS

HATS HAVE SOME OF THE POWERS local authorities would have if they still owned the housing, for example the same housing management powers; planning powers to develop land or property for commercial or residential use; and powers over roads, public health, the administration of grants, and the compulsory purchase of private sector property.

3.14 ACCESS TO PERSONAL FILES

TENANTS WILL HAVE A RIGHT of access to housing records held by HATs — under the Access to Personal Files Act 1987. (Note also that from April 1st 1989 this right also applies to tenants, or former tenants, of local authorities — and also applies to people who have applied for council housing, or have bought their homes from a council.)

3.15 THE LOCAL GOVERNMENT OMBUDSMAN

SCHEDULE 17, PARAGRAPH 19 OF THE 1988 Housing Act adds HATs to the list of authorities which are subject to investigation under the Local Government Act 1974.

4. Change of Landlord — Public Sector

INTRODUCTION

"Change of landlord" is only the last of a long line of labels for this scheme. Originally Government ministers called it *"Pick a Landlord"* or *"Tenants' Choice"*. The problem with such names was that the actual Bill made it clear that the scheme was to be structured around landlord applications. So finally they settled for a neutral title for the purposes of the Act, although Housing Corporation publicity refers to *"Tenants' Choice"*.

The essential aim of the scheme is the dismantling of council housing — an adjunct to the Right to Buy. It is notable that private tenants are not given the right to choose a council landlord. It is yet another part of the Government's overall policy of transferring the means of housing provision from the public to the private sector.

The Government has attempted to allay tenants' fears of loss of rights under the *"Change of Landlord"* scheme, by the introduction of *"pre-selection"* and *"approval"* safeguards to cover would-be landlords; and a *"Tenants' Guarantee"*. But as with so much else connected with this Act, these are seen by many of the people likely to be affected by the scheme as remedies to problems which the Act itself has created.

A key feature of the transfer of public sector housing into other hands is the relationship between the *"Change of Landlord"* scheme, which involves parts of a public sector landlord's housing stock being transferred to another body, and *"Voluntary Transfers"* which involve transfer of the entire housing stock. The formal relationship is covered in the Guide. In many areas voluntary transfer proposals are being made as a means of pre-empting the *"Change of Landlord"* scheme, though the DoE has stated that the Secretary of State will not normally give consent to a voluntary disposal unless tenants have been given a chance to consider transfer under the *"Change of Landlord"* scheme. In areas where tenants have rejected voluntary transfer proposals, or where none has been made, the *"Change of Landlord"* scheme is likely to gradually chip away the local authority sector.

This scheme was introduced by PART IV of the Act, which came into force on April 5th 1989. In the Act itself it is called "Change of Landlord". However, in Government publicity it is called "Tenant's Choice". Landlord bodies will be able to apply to take over public sector housing ranging from large blocks of property to a single house. These landlords must be approved by the Housing Corporation and will be subject to a pre-selection procedure. They can take over housing where there are secure tenants of a local council, a New Town, a Housing Action Trust, or the Development Board of Rural Wales. The scheme is subject to a tenant voting system. A 50% eligible voter turnout is required for a transfer to go through. Under this voting system an abstention counts as a "yes" vote. In effect a take-over will go ahead unless more than half the tenants eligible to vote actually vote against it. A tenant who votes "no" will stay as a tenant of the old landlord. Tenants who transfer to the new landlord become assured tenants.

There has been a lot of confusion about the relationship between "Change of Landlord" and "Voluntary Transfer". The answer is that "Change of Landlord" is governed by Part IV of the 1988 Housing Act, and involves bids for sections of public housing stock. "Voluntary Transfers" arise out of powers contained in the 1986 Housing and Planning Act, under which local authorities (after consulting tenants — which in effect means a ballot) can try to transfer their entire housing stock to a new or existing housing association (or consortium of housing associations).

The essential difference in the voting system between the two types of scheme is that whereas under "Tenants' Choice" a "no" vote means the tenant having a right to remain with the old landlord, this is not the case under "Voluntary Transfer".

The question of what happens if an outside landlord body intends to make a bid for part of the housing stock at the same time as the present landlord is trying to transfer all its stock to another body, has been answered by a joint statement from the Department of the Environment and the Housing Corporation: "Arrangements for Interaction Between Tenants' Choice and other powers for Transferring Public Sector Housing." — published on March 22nd 1989. This statement sets out the principle that — ". . . only one transfer proposal . . . should be able to proceed at any one time, and must be allowed to run its course before another transfer proposal affecting some or all of the same dwellings can be set in train." This does however beg the question of what is meant by "running its course".

The approach of the National Federation of Housing Associations to "Tenants' Choice" is that its member associations should only become involved in tenant transfer if there is genuine support by tenants as demonstrated in a positive ballot vote; if the local authority is not reasonably opposed to the proposal; and if resources are available to deal with long-term management, maintenance and repair needs of the homes in question. It has also said that associations should react to requests from tenants rather than initiate the "landlord driven" procedures of the Act without such contact having been made; and that associations should "remain committed" to full information, involvement and consultation with the local authority as the best possible means of securing support for the implementation of tenants' wishes "where these are genuinely attested".

4.1 THE BASIC SCHEME

A. CONTROL OVER THE SCHEME.

The English scheme is controlled by the Housing Corporation. The Welsh scheme is controlled by Housing for Wales (Tai Cymru). The 1988 Housing Act does not apply to "Tenants' Choice" in Scotland. The scheme there is controlled by Scottish Homes, a body set up by the 1988 Housing (Scotland) Act, which is the relevant legislation.

The Housing Corporation operates on the basis of 8 regional offices, each one of which has a Tenants' Transfer Manager. Under them there are Tenants' Transfer Officers. Its head office is in London. Housing for Wales has two offices. There is a North Wales regional office, but the main office is in Cardiff, and that is where the "Tenants' Choice Team" is based, which includes a Manager and an Officer.

Apart from the obligation on the Housing Corporation and Housing for Wales to conform to the 1976 Race Relations Act there are no clear rights of complaint or redress concerning actions of these bodies. There is no Ombudsperson or similar body. Complaints could be addressed to the Secretary of State for the Environment, and ultimately they might be susceptible to judicial review.

B. WHICH LANDLORD BODIES ARE ELIGIBLE TO TAKE OVER?

Housing associations (registered, non-registered), commercial landlords (companies, partnerships, or individuals), or tenant controlled bodies (tenants' co-operatives [not tenant-management co-operatives], neighbourhood housing associations, tenant companies) — approved by the Housing Corporation, will be able to take over the freehold of tenants' homes (of secure tenants, and also of long-leaseholders) owned by public sector landlords — meaning local authorities, New Towns, HATs, and the Development Board for Rural Wales. Tenant management will also be possible under the new landlord. Public sector landlords themselves cannot become approved bodies.

The position of charitable housing associations concerning the acquisition of tenanted housing under this scheme has been explained earlier in this Guide (see 2.20).

The Housing Corporation says it will provide support and practical help to tenants considering a take-over by a tenant controlled body. It says it will help tenants find expert professional advice in this regard. It also says that it may provide money to enable tenants' groups to employ independent advisors for financial or technical help, particularly concerning raising the money for the scheme and sorting out what repairs and improvements need to be carried out. This help might come from housing associations, secondary co-ops (which exist to support tenant-based initiatives), or private consultants. Essentially the provision of money to buy-in this help is entirely at the discretion of the Housing Corporation, and the Act does not go so far as to give tenants a right to choose the source of the help.

Tenant controlled bodies will have to seek approved landlord status from the Housing Corporation (or Housing for Wales), just like other landlord bodies. Like some others, they would also be eligible for registration by the Corporation.

C. WHICH TENANTS QUALIFY FOR THE SCHEME?

The issue of who does and does not qualify for the scheme is complicated — and we have tried to make the position clear below.

Not all tenants and occupants have full rights under the scheme.
There are three factors to consider:

1. The type of tenancy/occupancy,
2. Whether the flat, house or block can transfer, and
3. Whether a "lease-back" to the local authority is possible.

Tenants will not qualify for the scheme, and therefore not be entitled to a vote, if they live in housing:
● that they occupy under a contract of employment as part of their job.

- where the landlord only has a lease, not the freehold.
- owned by a county council.

Only "qualifying" tenants have to be consulted by the applicant landlord. Consultation culminates in a ballot (for the ballot procedures see 4.5 below).

Under Section 93 of the Act a qualifying tenant is a secure tenant (other than one who has to give up possession under a dated possession order, or one who is within certain categories excluded from the Right to Buy. We refer to both of these in more detail later on.)

The Act goes on to say, in Section 102, that those who have a right to vote are:- qualifying tenants (as above); and tenants in flats who have become long-leaseholders (e.g. under the Right to Buy) where the public sector landlord still has the freehold.

In both cases they have to have lived in that accommodation at the date the application was made and to have been in continuous occupation throughout the consultation period — (however, there is provision for temporary absence). Secure tenants with a dated court possession order against them do not have a vote.

Section 102 also says that additional categories of tenants who have to be consulted (and therefore have a vote) can be prescribed by Regulations under Section 100(2) or 102(c).

Additional categories of tenants with a right to be consulted.

Regulations were then made. SI 367 — the "Housing (Change of Landlord) Regulations 1989" — came into force on April 5th 1989. Regulation 8 defines those tenants prescribed under Section 100((2)(b). These tenants have to have lived in that accommodation throughout the consultation period.

- Situations where the application has not included a property but the present landlord says that the property should be transferred because it cannot otherwise be properly managed or maintained. There has to be a qualifying tenant, whose tenancy began before the date of the prospective landlord's application.

- Secure tenants who would have been qualifying tenants but for a dated possession order against them. To have the right to be consulted the tenant has to give the applicant landlord a certificate that the present landlord no longer intends to enforce the order. But the certificate has to be given before the last 21 days of the consultation period.

● Certain non-secure tenants housed temporarily by local authorities (homeless people housed pending enquiries, following intentional home-lessness decisions, or pending possible referral to other authorities; people taking up local employment; and students, to enable attendance at a designated educational course) where the fixed temporary term set by Schedule 1 of the 1985 Housing Act has run out and the occupant is still there. People in this situation have to give the applicant landlord a certificate that they have become secure tenants by the "effluxion of time" (i.e. a fixed-term has come to an end.) The same 21 day rule applies as above.

People who the local authority has placed in permanent accommodation following acceptance by the local authority of a full duty to house are legally secure tenants. Consequently they have a right, as secure tenants, to be consulted. This will be the case even if the local authority claims that it is temporary accommodation, provided that the tenant has self-contained accommodation.

● Statutory successors to a qualifying tenant, who give the applicant landlord a certificate of their succession. The same 21 day rule applies as above. People who have become successors after the consultation period has begun are included as long as they have observed the 21 day rule.

People entitled to a vote but whose homes cannot be leased-back to the old landlord, or excluded from an acquisition.

Regulation 15 of SI 367 defines those tenants prescribed under Section 102. It sets out 3 categories:

● Business tenants who are there on the application date and throughout the consultation period.

● Long-leaseholders where the property was not included in the application but the present landlord says that the property should be transferred because it cannot otherwise be properly managed or maintained. There has to be a qualifying tenant, but in such cases that tenant only has to have lived there since the present landlord's response notice (under Section 98(1)), not since the date of the prospective landlord's application.

An extra category of tenant entitled to a vote whose homes do qualify for lease-back or exclusion from an acquisition.

Regulation 15 specifies:

● Tenants whose tenancies were assigned to them by way of exchange, after the application date, by qualifying tenants whose own tenancies began before the application date but who had not voted. Because the tenancy itself has been transferred these people are themselves qualifying tenants, but they still have to give the applicant landlord a certificate of the assignment in order to gain the entitlement to vote. The same 21 day rule applies — as above.

The position of long-leaseholders.

Long-leaseholders in flats, where the Right to Buy has been exercised, will have a vote. But in every case where an acquisition goes ahead they will hold from the new freeholder, and are not eligible for lease-back to the old landlord — although their vote will count towards the collective decision by tenants.

Where a tenant has bought the freehold under the Right to Buy (i.e. a house) the Change of Landlord scheme cannot apply, by definition. Therefore in this context, other than in exceptional cases (where the local authority does not own the freehold of a house) the scheme only applies to flats bought under the Right to Buy.

Situations where tenants have no vote but where the freehold will transfer to the new landlord and whose homes will be leased-back to the old landlord.

Regulation 7 of SI 367 prescribes a number of categories of tenants of flats, who are not qualifying tenants — and therefore have no vote — but where the freehold will transfer to the new landlord, with a lease-back to the old landlord should the acquisition go ahead. They are as follows:

● Some non-secure tenants (living there on the application date) — but not business tenancies or long tenancies — under paragraphs 2 to 7, 10 or 11 of Schedule 1 to the 1985 Housing Act — e.g. among others, premises occupied in connection with employment; accommodation for homeless people housed under local authority duties to rehouse temporarily; and temporary accommodation during works.

● Secure tenants of flats, living there on the application date, who occupy the accommodation in the circumstances set out in paragraphs 5, 7, or 9 to 11 of Schedule 5 to the 1985 Housing Act (exceptions to the Right to Buy) — e.g. temporary accommodation for people taking up employment, or temporary accommodation during works.

● Secure tenants obliged, on the application date or some later date, to give up possession because they have a dated possession order against them — and who do not give the applicant landlord a certificate saying that the present landlord no longer intends to enforce the order against them. Note however that tenants who have a suspended possession order against them are not disqualified, and they do have a right to consultation and a vote.

● A statutory successor to a qualifying tenant, where the qualifying tenant has voted to continue as a tenant of the present landlord.

● A statutory successor to a qualifying tenant, when the qualifying tenant was living there on the application date but gave no notice of whether or not they wished to remain a tenant of the present landlord — and where the successor gives the applicant landlord a certificate of succession in the required time.

● A qualifying tenant who gives the applicant landlord a certificate, within the required time, that the tenancy has been assigned to him/her after the application date by way of exchange by a qualifying tenant whose tenancy began before the application date.

Note that leaseback is permanent in the case of sheltered accommodation, but in all other cases it lasts only until the end of the tenancy or succession to the tenancy. Note also that squatters, licensees, and sub-tenants (where the tenant is absent), will not have a right to be consulted. Their homes will be leased-back to the old landlord.

D. BUILDINGS EXCLUDED FROM THE SCHEME.

A potential landlord will not be able to bid for accommodation in the following circumstances:

● If there are two or more flats in the building, and more than half of them are occupied on the application date by non-qualifying secure tenants, e.g. tenants in sheltered accommodation. This would mean, for example, that where there is a block of ten flats, and six of them were occupied by secure tenants not eligible to vote, then the other four secure tenants who would otherwise be qualifying tenants will remain with the present landlord automatically.

● a house occupied on the application date by tenants who are not secure tenants.

● a house occupied on the application date by tenants who are secure tenants, but are among the groups already mentioned who are excluded from the Right to Buy.

● a building where all the occupants are long-leaseholders who have exercised the Right to Buy.

● if the building is primarily non-residential (e.g. a school or an office), unless closely associated with residential use of homes in the acquisition.

In addition — certain pleasure grounds, open spaces and burial grounds are excluded from the scheme if they are not part of a dwelling or let together with it.

An applicant might argue that some buildings should be taken over because they are reasonably required for occupation with homes taken over. This might apply to residential homes (including those geographically outside a local authority's area — as long as the old landlord has the freehold); day centres; community centres; tenants' halls; and nurseries. This is a complex issue. In effect, it would be up to the present landlord to argue on the basis of Sections 93, 95 and 98 that such buildings should not transfer. However where the building was by its nature residential the present landlord might have more difficulty in retaining it.

E. EMPTY HOUSING.

For the purposes of the Act "empty" is taken to mean having no qualifying tenant in the building, (as opposed to the flat).

Buildings with no qualifying tenants, but where one or all of the following groups are in occupation, would seem to be excluded (i.e. treated as empty):

● long leaseholders
● insecure tenants
● licensees
● squatters
● people with dated court possession orders against them
● Right to Buy exemptions

An applicant landlord can take over some properties with vacant possession:

● flats vacant on the application date in blocks which are taken over.

● flats lived in on the application date by licensees or trespassers in buildings where there is at least one qualifying tenant. The present landlord would have the responsibility to evict. In a written answer to a Parliamentary Question (January 26th 1989) Junior Environment Minister David Trippier said that where a local authority had allocated a flat to a person on an estate which was subject to a bid from another landlord, vacant possession would be given to the landlord on transfer. He said — "Such lettings will therefore be temporary and will not involve the transfer of dwellings over a tenant's or licensee's head. Existing landlords will be required to make the temporary nature of any such lettings clear at the time to the tenants or licensees."

● flats and houses which have become empty between the application date and the take-over date.

The position of existing tenant management co-operatives.

Existing tenant management co-ops, with a public sector landlord, can be taken over if the co-op agrees, but it is a case of all or nothing. An applicant landlord cannot take-over part only. The co-op property can constitute only one part of the property taken over.

F. PROCEDURES.

The Act itself outlines some of the procedures, but many important details are left to a variety of papers and guidance notes from either the Government or the Housing Corporation. The Housing Corporation's "Tenants' Choice — How It Works" summarises the procedures. It was not published until May 1989. It replaces two earlier Housing Corporation booklets (published in January 1989) — a small green one for tenants called "Tenants' Choice: Your Power to Choose", and a small orange one for prospective landlords called — "Tenants' Choice: Becoming an Approved Landlord." The equivalent in Wales is called "The Path to Tenants' Choice." The Department of the Environment and the Welsh Office have published a booklet summarising the scheme. It is called simply "Tenants' Choice".

The Housing Corporation has produced a number of other publications:-

"The Choice is Yours" is an illustrated booklet. It is sometimes called the 'Pattern Book.' It gives an outline explanation of the types of alternative landlord (including tenant run bodies), and suggests questions tenants should ask of them. It was published in April 1989. In Wales there is "The Guide to Tenants' Choice in Wales", and a leaflet, "Tenants' Choice". Then there is "Questions You Should Ask — Advice on the Questions Tenants Should Put to Landlords", which was published in May 1989. The equivalent in Wales is "Questions for New Landlords". Another one is "The Options" published in April 1989. This is a small yellow leaflet, giving very general information. There is also "Keeping Tenants Informed" (May 1989). It is called the same in Wales. It contains the information that prospective landlords must give to tenants.

In addition the Department of the Environment and the Welsh Office ran a newspaper advertising campaign in March 1989, under the heading — "Council Tenants — Who should manage your Home? You decide." Housing for Wales has a publication without a Housing Corporation equivalent: "Tenant Owned Associations", which is information about how tenants can set up their own organisation to take over the ownership and running of their estate. Other Government and Housing Corporation (and Housing for Wales) publications are noted in the relevant sections below.

G. HOUSING CORPORATION POWERS ON PROVIDING INFORMATION TO TENANTS AND LANDLORDS.

Under Section 106 (which came into force on January 15th 1989) the Housing Corporation has powers to give information, advice and assistance to potential new landlords, and can charge them for it. Help to tenants will be free.

H. HOUSING CORPORATION (AND HOUSING FOR WALES) POWERS TO PROVIDE LEGAL ASSISTANCE TO TENANTS.

This help (which the tenant has to ask for, and the Corporation has discretion over) can include advice, arranging arbitration, arranging for the giving of advice, assistance or representation by a solicitor or barrister, and any other form of assistance, to deal with disputes on matters of principle, complexity or any other consideration. The Corporation will have a right to recoup its costs from any costs or settlement won by the tenant.

4.2 AN ALTERNATIVE LANDLORD — STAGE ONE: APPROVAL

A. WHO APPROVES LANDLORDS.

Under Section 94 (which came into force on January 15th 1989) landlords will have to be approved (for the purposes of general or particular take-overs) by the Housing Corporation.

There is "specific" approval, which relates to specific addresses in an area. There is also "general" approval, which means general permission to operate as an approved landlord in a particular area (e.g. a county) or a number of areas — but if this is obtained the landlord body still has to obtain "specific" approval in order to make an application.

B. CRITERIA SET BY THE HOUSING CORPORATION.

In January 1989 the Housing Corporation published a big orange booklet —
"Tenants' Choice: Criteria for Landlord Approval and Guidance Notes for
Applicants." The Welsh equivalent has the same title. This contains full
details of the standards which the Housing Corporation requires from an
applicant landlord body. Appendix 1 lists the criteria for approval (these are
explained in detail in the main body of the document). Appendix 2 contains
the housing management guidance for bodies which are not registered
housing associations.

The criteria are:-

● **statutory requirements** (eligible bodies, payment, an agreement to
accept any additional undertakings);

● **status** (can be incorporated, unincorporated, or individual/s);

● **control and accountability** (responsible, likely effectiveness, a proper
management structure, declaration that any outside control or influence not
prejudicial to approval terms);

● **financial requirements** (must show that it operates or will operate on a
sound and proper financial basis);

● **managerial efficiency** (access to skills and efficiency regarding acquisition, management, and maintenance — from its own staff or from elsewhere
— to a high standard and to serve the best interests of tenants);

● **proposed level and area of activity** (consideration will be related to the
body's size and resources);

● **equal opportunities** (in policies and procedures — according to the
Corporation's statutory duty under Section 71 of the 1976 Race Relations Act
— "to eliminate unlawful racial discrimination and to promote equality of
opportunity, and good relations between persons of different racial
groups";

● **other requirements**
– not to apply to acquire property under the scheme if the Corporation asks
  them not to;
– to submit to the pre-selection process;
– to keep tenants and the Corporation informed at all key stages, and all
  parties in the event of withdrawal;
– to give all formal consultation material to the Corporation for checking
  against the approval criteria and other undertakings;
– to obtain the Corporation's approval for the appointment of (and the
  contract terms of) the independent teller;
– to stick to formal consultation terms offered to tenants;

- to keep confidential all information on tenants, and only disclose it to third parties where necessary for the purpose of pursuing an application;
- to retain dwellings acquired, for letting at rents within the reach of people in low-paid employment;
- rents and other charges to be generally consistent;
- to comply with the Corporation's Management Guidance;
- not to try to take over any house occupied by a tenant who voted to stay with the present landlord, but who left after the price for the acquisition was finally fixed;
- not to use the assured tenancy possession Ground 6 (the redevelopment ground). If they need vacant possession to do works, they will have to offer suitable alternative accommodation under Ground 9;
- to give the Corporation any further information asked for;
- within 6 months of the end of its financial year, to give the Corporation its audited annual accounts, and an annual return related to its activities under this scheme;
- to give the Corporation 4 weeks notice of any proposed change to its objects and powers, (which may require the Corporation's consent under Section 19 of the 1985 Housing Associations Act); and to give 4 weeks notice of changes of membership of the governing body, of managerial and executive staff, or of address;
- to observe all these requirements at all times in the future.

In addition, to qualify for **general approval** the applicant has to show that it has at least 2 years experience of managing "social rented housing" in the manner described in the Corporation's management guidance; a high degree of financial strength, and evidence of financial stability; and the managerial capacity to cope with the anticipated growth in the levels and areas of its "Tenants' Choice" landlord activity.

Strangely, housing management guidance for registered housing associations was not included in the "Tenants' Choice: Criteria for Landlord Approval and Guidance Notes for Applicants" document. That was left to a January 1989 Housing Corporation document called —
"The Tenants' Guarantee: Guidance on the Management by Registered Housing Associations of Housing Accommodation let on Assured Tenancies under the Housing Act 1988." (This guidance is in effect supplemented by a Government Circular — "Access to Housing Association Housing" — which sets out their duties on meeting housing demand and concerning allocation.)

The Housing Corporation has published separate management guidance documents on — fully mutual housing co-operatives; almshouse charities;

providing special needs housing in shared accommodation and hostels; and letting on long leases, including shared ownership.

C. HOW LANDLORD BODIES APPLY FOR APPROVED LANDLORD STATUS.

The Housing Corporation has published two forms. One, Form TC1, is 20 pages long and is for bodies which are not registered housing associations. The second, Form TC2, is 14 pages long and is for registered housing associations.

D. SANCTIONS AGAINST LANDLORDS IF THEY DO NOT STICK TO CRITERIA.

Landlords can lose approved body status if they do not adhere to these criteria. But any revocation would not affect the right to carry on managing completed Change of Landlord take-overs. At the time of writing (May 1989) the document on revocation procedures is still awaited.

As part of the approval process the applicant will have to take out a contract, i.e. between the landlord body and the Housing Corporation. This is called a "Deed under Seal" which will tie the landlord body to the Criteria, and to the Management Guidance. This means that there will be a 'locus standii' between the Housing Corporation and the landlord body, rather than between the tenant and the landlord body. This enables the Housing Corporation to act directly against the landlord in the case of a breach. For detailed comment on remedies see our paragraph 4.7(a) later in this Guide.

E. TENANTS MANAGEMENT COOPS TENANTS WANTING APPROVAL.

If tenants of homes subject to a Tenant Management Cooperative Agreement wish to seek approval they will have to include all the homes covered by that agreement in any application they make. And only that accommodation can be included in the application.

F. OTHER TENANTS WANTING TO BECOME APPROVED BODIES.

The Act is silent on the position of tenants in general who may wish to join together to make an application. Informal as this arrangement is, they are free to make an application for approval to the Housing Corporation.

4.3 AN ALTERNATIVE LANDLORD — STAGE TWO: PRE-SELECTION

THERE ARE TWO WAYS in which the process of transfer to a new landlord will begin. One is where tenants actively seek to replace their present landlord by persuading another, existing, landlord body to take over — or to propose take over by some form of tenant managed body. The other is where an outside landlord body actively seeks to persuade the tenants that it should be allowed to take over. In effect the Housing Corporation (or Housing for Wales) has two distinct roles in this regard. The first is to make available sufficient information to enable tenants to achieve their objectives. The second is to administer a machinery which is capable of determining which, among competing bodies, has the most tenant support for the bid to go to a vote.

Where there is more than one potential applicant the Housing Corporation will hold a preliminary competition between them. But if there is only one potential applicant the Housing Corporation will try to establish, by way of an initial informal consultation with tenants (an informal test of tenant opinion), whether that body has the 10% initial support in principle from tenants which is necessary before the Corporation can give clearance for a formal application to be made.

Preselection procedures are set out in "Tenants' Choice: The Informal Competition — Housing Corporation Guidance on the Informal Consultation of Tenants" published by the Housing Corporation in May 1989. This document says that the Corporation intends that tenants themselves should "be in control of the pace at which the process proceeds," "which prospective landlords they wish to see," and "the timing and nature of discussions involving their existing public sector landlord".

It also says that although the Corporation wishes to deal with "Tenants' Choice "in an entirely open fashion" it will "respect tenant and landlord insistence on confidentiality during the initial exploratory discussion stage . . ."

The procedures are outlined as follows:

a. The initial contact between the Housing Corporation and an interested tenants' group or alternative approved landlord.

If tenants or leaseholders contact the Corporation and have no particular solution in mind they will be sent (if they wish) an information pack, including an explanatory booklet and a note on what kinds of landlords might be available. If landlord bodies make unsolicited approaches to tenants, these tenants are asked to tell their present landlord and the Corporation.

If a landlord body tells the Corporation it is interested in a property then the Corporation will "in due course" put it in contact with the tenants (see c. later); try to identify other possible new landlords; and "if possible and appropriate, take the lead in arranging an informal competition".

Potential take-over landlords are warned that approaching tenants or the present landlord direct could prejudice approval or the terms eventually on offer. They are advised to keep the Corporation informed and involved from the beginning.

Some potential take-over landlords can take part in the informal competition prior to approval. Prospective resident controlled landlords such as "embryonic" co-ops, and Neighbourhood Housing Associations — "are unlikely to apply for approval unless they are successful in the informal competition." The document also says that the same will "often apply to existing alternative landlords".

b. The consequent informal discussions between the Housing Corporation and tenants.

The Corporation will advise groups of tenants (or individuals), and arrange contact with existing or prospective approved landlords — regardless of the size of the possible transfer. If a group of tenants who have been sent the information pack want to take matters further the Corporation will give a "presentation" to the tenants at a meeting. It will do the same if it has received a "serious" approach from an approved landlord or one which is "a likely candidate for approval". The presentation will involve an explanation of (and objective factual information about) alternative landlord options, and information on requirements and procedures. It will also say that staying with the present landlord is an option. Information will not be presented "on behalf of or advocating any specific landlord or landlord type".

If this initial meeting is with tenants' representatives rather than an open meeting, the Corporation will want to be satisfied that arrangements will be made for all affected tenants to be given an opportunity to make their views known. To help achieve this the Corporation has a discretionary power to help (which can include financial assistance) in the production of information leaflets to be distributed, or help with other appropriate publicity. It may ask for more than one meeting before matters are allowed to move on to the next stage.

c. The introduction of tenants to alternative landlords, and their presentations to the interested parties.

If tenants wish, the Corporation will then provide more detailed information — "about all landlords likely to offer the services that the tenants are interested in," and specific introductions could be made. But the Corporation will "also introduce at this stage landlords which had previously expressed an interest". If tenants and a specific landlord are already in contact, the Corporation will now "try to introduce possible alternatives".

If tenants want to set up their own landlord, possibly a Co-op, or a Neighbourhood Housing Association, the Corporation will discuss with them training, support with publicity, start-up grants, and where necessary will introduce them to other support agencies. If tenants are very strongly in favour of a tenant-controlled or other specific option, the Corporation may decide not to introduce possible alternative competitors — but the Corporation has to adhere to guidance. The Corporation is debarred in its "Tenants' Choice" activities from assisting the setting-up of Tenant Management Co-ops under continuing local authority landlordship.

Otherwise landlord presentations, involving response to questions from tenants, will be arranged. A booklet will be published suggesting the types of questions to ask. The Corporation will propose that the tenants ask the same questions of their present landlord. The Corporation insists on being notified, and having the right to be represented at all meetings between a potential landlord and tenants or their representatives.

Potential landlords will be free to circulate tenants with "leaflets or information". The Corporation says "it may" be in that body's interest to consult it on content — as it might form the basis of what will become a legally binding offer. In addition the material given to tenants must be consistent with the terms of approval for landlords. If the material which forms part of the later formal consultation is inconsistent with this earlier material it must be highlighted and explained clearly. All information must be factually correct, and in an appropriate form (including alternative languages, braille or audio tape) where there is a "significant foreseeable need". Copies have to be sent to the Corporation. Also the Corporation wants potential landlords to state clearly the source and status of information given to tenants — to "avoid confusion" in the context where the present landlord is probably also calling meetings for tenants and producing "information leaflets".

d. The Housing Corporation's test of tenant opinion

When the Corporation is satisfied that all tenants potentially affected have had adequate information on the principle of transfer and what is on offer, it will notify the tenants, the present landlord, and the potential landlords involved, how it intends to test tenant opinion. If satisfied that representatives have been mandated by properly arranged and advertised meetings, the Corporation will accept their advice. If in other cases there is a clear indication of agreement on a specific alternative landlord (in other words evidence of positive support for a particular proposition, widely publicised among affected tenants) there will be no further testing. But if there is doubt, or evidence of substantial disagreement, the Corporation will test opinion by personal contact, public or group meetings, or survey. The decision on method rests with the Corporation, but there will be consultation with tenants, and the present and potential landlords.

Before a specific landlord body can start the statutory application procedure it has to cross two hurdles. It has to have at least 10% in-principle support from the tenants affected, for itself as opposed to a competitor potential alternative landlord. But it also has to demonstrate that it has at least 10% in-principle support for its application.

It would appear that the guidance gives the Housing Corporation unlimited discretion concerning the procedures to be adopted.

The Corporation will make the results of these tests available to all the parties, and any other interested groups.

e. Moving to the application stage.

If the 10% requirements have been met, the Corporation will write to the potential landlord saying they are free to proceed to an application. If such a body were to apply to the present landlord without this notice it would be in breach of its approval conditions and would risk having it revoked. Unsuccessful bodies will also be written to.

The Corporation will then open discussions with the successful body on the next steps, and timing. That body could at this stage still decide not to proceed (as it can much later, even after winning a ballot).

If the body which decides to go ahead has not yet been approved by the Corporation, then it has to apply promptly for approval. Once approved it will have to apply equally promptly to take over the housing. Undue delay in the latter could mean its approved status being reviewed.

In the case of a tenant-controlled landlord being the preferred option the Corporation will timetable with the tenants the tying-up of any outstanding arrangements, including a possible formal application for the Corporation's assistance, if such an application has not yet been made.

Once this 10% support issue has been resolved it is too late for any other body to put in a bid.

4.4 AN ALTERNATIVE LANDLORD — STAGE THREE: THE APPLICATION

IF A POSSIBLE ALTERNATIVE LANDLORD body has passed through the approval and pre-selection hurdles it can then apply to the present landlord.

The procedure is set out in the Act. The various prescribed forms are set out in "The Housing (Change of Landlord) (Prescribed Forms) Regulations 1989, SI No. 374." These regulations allow forms "substantially the same as" these forms to be used.

FORM 1 — THE APPLICATION

In order to exercise the 'Right to acquire' under Section 96(1) the prospective landlord has to make an application on Form 1 — "Notice claiming the right to acquire under Part IV." The information asked for includes the name and address of the old and the prospective landlord, evidence of the applicant's approved landlord status, the addresses of any homes involved which are subject to an approved tenant co-operative management agreement, and a plan showing each building it is hoped to acquire.

The applicant has to notify the tenants affected, individually, in writing, that it has sent Form 1.

FORM 2 — INFORMATION FROM PRESENT LANDLORD TO POTENTIAL LANDLORD

The present landlord then has 4 weeks to give the applicant on Form 2 — "Notice specifying information for the applicant" — the names and addresses of all tenants (including sub-tenants) and licensees in the properties involved. This includes people who have exercised the Right to Buy flats. In addition there has to be a note on the "general nature" of each tenancy or licence — i.e whether it is a tenancy or licence; whether it is a secure tenancy under the 1985 Housing Act, and if it is, whether it is a qualifying tenancy under the Change of Landlord scheme; if it is not a secure tenancy, whether it is a business tenancy, long lease or not secure for some other reason; whether it is periodic or fixed-term; when it was granted; and, if applicable, its expiry date.

Prospective landlords (if successful) can take over some properties with vacant possession — flats vacant on the application date in blocks taken over; flats lived in on the application date by licensees or trespassers in blocks containing qualifying tenants; and flats and houses which become empty between the application date and take-over date.

It should be noted here that after the application date the present landlord is not permitted to grant a secure tenancy in property which an applicant proposes to take over. And it would seem that if the present landlord had granted any other tenancy or licence on that property then if the new landlord wished it the present landlord would have to get the occupant out before the take-over. If the new landlord were to be left with the task the old landlord would end up having to pay any costs involved in evicting.

When the 4 weeks are up the applicant can visit any empty property involved, and has a right to get from the present landlord, and copy, all documents "reasonably required". These include rent and rent arrears records, and tenants' files. (But note that arrears debts will not be transferred from the old landlord to the new landlord. The local authority would have to pursue them as a civil debt, through the courts if necessary.)

FORM 3 — ISSUES THE PRESENT LANDLORD WANTS TO TAKE UP

The present landlord has 12 weeks from the Form 1 application to spell out any specific concerns it has relating to the properties involved in the application. It does so on Form 3 — "Notice stating landlord's proposals as to property proposed to be acquired." The information can cover:

● Buildings and property it feels should be excluded from acquisition because there are no "qualifying tenants" in them;
● Property it feels should be excluded because it is not reasonably required for occupation with buildings proposed to be acquired; or that it is property reasonably required for occupation but which is involved with buildings and property which it feels should be excluded under the first group;
● Property it feels should be excluded because it is precluded by Section 95 — parts are occupied for business purposes and that part amounts to more than half the total internal floor area without common parts. And property needed for occupation with that excluded property;
● Property it feels should be excluded because it is subject to an approved co-operative management agreement;
● Property the present landlord wants to be taken over on the ground that it

cannot otherwise be reasonably managed or maintained;

● Rights the present landlord wants to retain over property included in the acquisition on the ground that they are necessary for the proper management or maintenance of land to be retained by the landlord;

● Proposals for the terms of the sale (conveyance) — subject to the requirements of Regulation 19 of, and Schedule 4 to, the Housing (Change of Landlord) Regulations 1989 (SI 367).

The applicant has to notify the tenants affected, in writing, that it has sent Form 3.

The applicant has 4 weeks from the date Form 3 was served to respond in writing to the present landlord.

If there is no agreement between the parties disputes can be sorted out by an agreed adjudicator, or failing that, by the Secretary of State.

FORM 4 — THE PRESENT LANDLORD SETS THE SALE PRICE

Once the present landlord has met the requests, or any dispute has been sorted out, the present landlord has to tell the applicant the sale price. In some cases, instead of receiving money from the applicant, the old landlord will pay the new landlord what has been called a 'dowry' to take on the property — this is now officially called the 'disposal cost'.

Form 4: "Notice specifying landlord's purchase price or disposal cost" is used for this purpose. It has to be served within 8 weeks of having served Form 3, or of a resolution of any dispute. This is the notice required by Section 99 of the Act.

Service of Form 4 marks the beginning of the consultation period, which runs for 14 weeks. See 4.5 below for details of the consultation process.

The proposed purchase price or disposal cost is the amount which on the application date the landlord considers the property would realise if sold on the open market by a willing vendor, subject to the assumptions set out in Section 99(2): i.e. vacant possession save for existing tenancies; the rights and burdens of the landlords remain the same; only approved bodies or bodies fulfilling the criteria for approval, as bidders; the applicant would in a reasonable period carry out works sufficient to fulfil the landlord's repairing obligations; and properties whose tenants end up staying with the present landlord are included in the valuation — adjustments being made at the time of any transfer of ownership.

The applicant has 4 weeks, from the time Form 4 has been served, to write to the present landlord concerning anything in the notice that it finds unacceptable.

Advice on valuation — "Valuation Liaison Group Professional Guidance Note. No. 2, Section IV — Change of Landlord: Secure Tenants — Part IV of the 1988 Housing Act." — was circulated to local authorities on February 28th in England, and March 31st in Wales.

Disputes on valuation will be dealt with by the District Valuer, under procedures set out in Regulation 5 and Schedule 2 of the Housing (Change of Landlord) Regulations following rules which will be set out.

In January 1989 the Department of the Environment and the Welsh Office issued a consultation paper concerning changes for housing subsidy following disposals. "Residual Debt Subsidy" (RDS), in respect of loan charges on any notional residual debt related to the homes sold, will be paid by the Exchequer on the following bases:

In England it will be paid at a rate of 75% of the loan charges, for sales under "Tenants' Choice", Right to Buy, and where there are individual sales. For all voluntary sales to other landlords the rate will be 90%. In Wales the rate will be 90% in all these cases. Where a Housing Action Trust is proposed the Government intends that any losses caused by the disposal, which are not covered by subsidy entitlement following disposal, will be met by the Exchequer by means of a "safety net" — in other words, there will be 100% subsidy. The paper says — "The idea is to ensure that no additional costs resulting from the transfer of the stock to a HAT should fall on the remaining tenants or ratepayers in the form of rent or rate increases."

4.5 AN ALTERNATIVE LANDLORD — STAGE FOUR: THE BALLOT

ONCE THE PURCHASE PRICE OR DISPOSAL COST is known the applicant has to consult all qualifying tenants. Details of consultation are contained in Part VI of the Housing (Change of Landlord) Regulations 1989 — SI No. 367. Balloting procedures are set out in Regulations 14 to 17 and Schedule 3 of the Housing (Change of Landlord) Regulations 1989 — SI No. 367. Further explanation is given in paras 21 to 35 of Annex A of Circular 11/89.

The applicant will have to "make all reasonable efforts" to consult all tenants, in writing "in clear and straightforward language", including — "where there is a significant foreseeable demand from tenants by whom written English is unlikely to be readily comprehended . . . for those tenants material in an alternative language or medium, including, where appropriate, braille and audio tape recording". In addition in Wales it can be in English and Welsh.

If there are complaints about the misconduct or irregularity of an applicant during the consultation process, the question of redress is unclear. At the time of writing (May 1989) the details of the revocation procedure are still awaited.

The consultation period, which runs for 14 weeks, begins with Service of Form 4. (see above). Within 7 weeks of the beginning of the consultation period the applicant landlord has to serve on each eligible tenant (except those who say they could be away during the vote) specified information. This is listed in Schedule 3 of SI No. 367. We summarise this below. In theory the applicant could wait until the sixth week before consulting.

Note that there will be only one vote per dwelling. (This means that joint tenants will only get one vote between them.)

FORM 7 — THE VOTING FORM FOR TENANTS

The applicant landlord gives eligible tenants Form 7 — "Notice of Decision by Tenants". This is the voting form. The tenant can send it to the teller by post, or deliver it themselves. Joint tenants also use this form — in which case there are two options for its completion:- all the joint tenants can sign it; or one or more can sign it on behalf of the others. But in any case the cross for the vote can only be put in one box out of the two available — to continue as the tenant/s of the existing landlord, or to become tenant/s of the proposed new landlord.

FORM 6 — THE VOTING FORM FOR TENANTS WHO WILL BE AWAY

Where a tenant (not joint tenants) tells the applicant landlord that s/he will or is likely to be away for all or most of the consultation period, then that landlord body has to give the tenant Form 6: "Notice of Decision by Absentees." This is a voting paper. The tenant can send it to the applicant landlord by post, or deliver it themselves. The applicant landlord then hands it, unopened, to the independent teller. Tenants who are in the armed services will have facilities for postal voting.

In a written reply (February 14th 1989) to a Parliamentary Question the Government said that members of the armed forces who were affected will be enabled by regulations to cast an advance vote at any point in the 14-week consultation period if they expect to be absent during the vote itself. Contact will be made by the independent teller through the British Forces Post Office.

The Act requires that everyone who is eligible should be notified. Despite the fact that the original Consultation Paper on the scheme said that Regulations would deal with the issue of contacting people who are away temporarily, in fact they do not. However, the independent teller will have to use its best endeavours to ensure that contact is made with people who, for example, are in hospital; temporarily in a residential home; or in prison.

By the time this Guide is out the Department of the Environment will have published a document which at the time of writing we expect to be called: "The Tenants' Contract." It should say how the applicant landlord is to employ the independent teller for the ballot, and details of the ballot procedure.

The vote will be organised and counted by an independent teller, employed and paid by the applicant landlord. The Electoral Reform Society have said they are prepared to carry out this function, but the Government is seeking to involve other bodies as well. For each application the teller used will be subject to approval by the Housing Corporation (or Housing for Wales), and employment will be on the basis of a model contract — which is available from these bodies.

There will be a 7 to 10 day gap between the end of the information phase and the ballot phase. This will allow local authorities to put forward their own proposals.

The voting itself will take place over a 4 week period, followed by around 3 weeks during which the independent teller will try to persuade tenants who have not voted to do so. This 'chasing up period' has to be seen in the context of abstentions counting as "yes" votes, which means that if the "yes" votes and the abstentions add up to 50% or more then the abstainers will become tenants of the new landlord, whereas people who vote "no" will stay on as council tenants — as secure tenants under the Housing Act 1985, and keep all their rights. If more than 50% of eligible voters vote "no" then no-one goes over to the new landlord. If less than 50% of eligible tenants vote, the application cannot go ahead.

Circular 11/89 says — ". . . where people who were eligible to be consulted have died or ceased to be tenants of the flat or house concerned, their failure to vote should not be included in the final reckoning. Such tenants will not appear in either part of the calculation in considering whether the 50% turnout requirement is met, nor will they appear in considering whether a majority of eligible tenants has voted to remain with their current landlord." (paragraph 24)

Tenants will receive written information from both the applicant landlord and the independent teller.

INFORMATION THE APPLICANT LANDLORD HAS TO GIVE TO ELIGIBLE TENANTS

In the first 7 weeks of the consultation period the applicant landlord has to make an offer of new tenancy terms in the appropriate language or media (there are special arrangements for service of this information where the tenant has said s/he will be away.) The terms have to be consistent with terms set out in Schedule 3 of SI. 367. These are listed below, and a draft has to be given to the Housing Corporation (or Housing for Wales) to confirm that it covers all the matters required by the regulations, the approval criteria, and undertakings given by the applicant landlord.

THE OFFER OF TENANCY TERMS BY APPLICANT LANDLORDS — REQUIREMENTS OF SCHEDULE 3, HOUSING (CHANGE OF LANDLORD) REGULATIONS 1989 — SI No. 367.

This information will be in two parts -

A. A statement on the applicant's offer (or non-offer) to secure tenants, on the following matters:

● how, if at all, the terms offered differ from the tenant's existing secure tenancy;
● the rent and any service charge which will be payable under the proposed tenancy, review procedures, the frequency of review, and any proposed limit on increases;
● the tenant's entitlement to take in lodgers, to sub-let part, or to part with possession of part of the accommodation;
● the tenant's entitlement to improve the accommodation;
● the applicant's arrangements to ensure tenants are informed of those proposals which will affect them — and arrangements for tenants to make their views known to the applicant before it makes decisions based on those proposals;
● the repairing obligations of the applicant landlord and the tenant (including common parts, and the making good of structural defects);
● any repairs (including the making good of structural defects) the applicant

proposes to carry out — and completion times;

● the applicant's arrangements for assessing repair and maintenance works (including how often visits will be made to assess need, and arrangements for tenants to notify need);

● the time within which the applicant undertakes to carry out emergency works and other works;

● the tenant's entitlement concerning mutual exchanges;

● any arbitration arrangements the applicant will make concerning disputes arising from the tenancy, or between tenants of property acquired by the applicant;

● whether the applicant landlord's consent is required for any purpose (and when it is to be withheld).

This statement also has to include an address and telephone number for further information and assistance from the applicant; and a statement that the Housing Corporation (or Housing for Wales) may give information, advice and assistance to tenants.

B. General information.

● that it is served according to regulations prescribed under Section 102(1);

● that it comes from the applicant, to enable the tenant to decide whether to stay as a tenant of the present landlord or become a tenant of the applicant landlord;

● that the teller will send a ballot form and an explanation of the voting process;

● the role of the teller;

● the voting position for joint tenants;

● the effect of Section 103(6) — which says that an abstention counts as a "yes" vote;

● the circumstances in which the transfer may take place;

● the circumstances in which the tenant will become a tenant of the applicant landlord;

● what becoming a tenant of the applicant will mean to secure tenants, tenants under long tenancies, and business tenants;

● in the event of the applicant taking over — when a tenant would have the right to refer a demand for a higher rent to a Rent Assessment Committee;

● rights the tenant would have concerning service charges;

● that the information coming from the teller will tell each tenant the nature of the present tenancy;

● the applicant's allocations policy, including special provision for housing difficulties experienced by particular groups including elderly people, people from ethnic minorities, people suffering domestic violence, people with physical or mental disability and those caring for people with such a disability, and any arrangements it will maintain to facilitate the move by its tenants to other accommodation;

● proposals (if any) for day to day management — including numbers, location and responsibilities of management staff.

The applicant landlord also has to employ an independent teller to conduct the ballot of tenants' views.

INFORMATION THE INDEPENDENT TELLER HAS TO GIVE TO ELIGIBLE TENANTS

Between 7 and 10 days after the applicant landlord's offer to the tenant the teller has to give every eligible tenant a ballot form (Form 7). It has to be accompanied by explanations of:

● the teller's independent role;
● the voting options;
● the consequences for tenants of each option (including an abstention);
● the circumstances in which a transfer may or may not proceed;
● the position of joint tenants, who have one vote between them;
● the confidential nature of the ballot process;
● advice on how to complete the ballot form and by when;
● a contact address and telephone number in case of queries.

In addition there must be a brief explanation of the nature of this material in a range of languages, and advice that people who do not understand should seek help.

If the application lapses, or is withdrawn for any reason, that landlord body is barred from re-applying for any or all of the same property without a further authorisation from the Corporation. Authorisation will not be given without further discussion between the Corporation, affected tenants or their representatives, and the existing public sector landlord.If the application falls, through lack of a 50% turnout, or because there is insufficient tenant support (even with abstentions counting as "yes" votes), that landlord body is barred from re-applying for any or all of the same property without a further authorisation from the Corporation.

In such cases a further informal competition will always be held. "In order to avoid vexatious repeated applications, the Corporation will require clear evidence, before permitting the same landlord to apply again, that tenant opinion or other relevant circumstances have changed sufficiently to give a reasonable prospect of adequate tenant support being demonstrated in the statutory ballot. For this reason, a threshold of support greater than the 10% ... will normally be required for the same landlord to re-apply. The Corporation will discuss with tenants and the existing and proposed landlords both the threshold and the method of assessing tenant support before reaching a decision."

4.6 PROCEDURES AFTER THE BALLOT

ONCE THE BALLOT HAS BEEN HELD a successful applicant can still decide not to go ahead with a take-over, in which case the tenants affected have to be informed, individually, in writing within two weeks.

FORM 5 — WHERE THE APPLICANT LANDLORD DECIDES TO GO AHEAD

If the applicant does decide to go ahead with the take-over, then within 2 weeks of the end of the consultation period it has to notify the present landlord on Form 5 — "Notice of intention to proceed with an acquisition under Part IV."

This notification has to contain:

● the names and addresses of tenants who have voted against the transfer;
● a list of excluded houses;
● a list of flats the successful applicant will have to lease back to the present landlord (and the proposed terms of the leases);
● how the lists in these categories were established;
● the total purchase price or disposal cost of the property to be acquired.

Where there is a purchase price (rather than a disposal cost), Section 103 of the 1988 Housing Act allows the new landlord to enter into a clawback arrangement, called a "prescribed covenant", to pay parts of that purchase price from future receipts when properties taken over are subsequently sold — and in the meantime for the acquiring purchase price to be reduced accordingly. The covenant applies for 15 years after transfer to receipts from all future sales to sitting tenants, whether under the Right to Buy or otherwise. The new landlord can use Form 5 to take up the option to enter into a prescribed covenant. The applicant landlord would covenant to pay the old landlord 65% of gross receipts from sales, or another percentage agreed between them. Any reduction in the purchase price for the transfer would be decided by the District Valuer.

Note that long leaseholders (or business tenants) of flats who voted to stay with their present landlord will not — under lease-back arrangements — continue as tenants of that landlord. Instead they will hold the tenancy from the new landlord, who is the new freeholder.

On receipt of Form 5 the old landlord has 2 weeks to respond in writing if anything is disputed. There is no appeal as such. Presumably the old landlord would have to go to court if it thought that the procedures had been illegal.

After Form 5 has been received (or after a dispute has been resolved) formal transfer has to take place. The old landlord has to convey the fee simple estate of the property, (i.e. freehold) subject to any retained rights. The new landlord grants any leases back to the old landlord, where appropriate. Tenants who voted "no" will stay with the old landlord. Tenants who voted "yes", and those who abstained, will become tenants of the new landlord.

Within one week of the transfer (completion) the new landlord has to inform the tenants affected in writing of the transfer itself, and the terms under which it has taken place.

Where an applicant wanted to take over a flat but the tenant voted to stay with the old landlord, the applicant takes over the freehold of the building and leases the flat back to the old landlord. So the tenant remains as a tenant of the old landlord. But if the tenancy ends (i.e. the tenant or a successor leaves, or dies) the leaseback arrangement is ended and the new landlord then controls that flat. A maisonette is considered to be a flat.

Where an applicant wanted to take over a house but the tenant voted to stay with the old landlord, the old landlord keeps the freehold, and the tenant remains the tenant of the old landlord. If the tenant leaves, that landlord still decides what happens to the house.

4.7 TENANCY RIGHTS AFTER TRANSFER

a. Tenancy status after transfer — and other rights.

Tenants whose homes are transferred to the new landlord will no longer be secure tenants (under the Housing Act 1985.) Instead they will be assured tenants (not assured shorthold tenants) under the new Housing Act. They will lose some of their Housing Act 1985 Tenants' Charter rights — succession rights would be much weaker; the right to be consulted would be lost; and there would be no right to participate in the Tenants' Exchange Scheme, or the National Mobility Scheme. At the time of writing (May 1989) plans are afoot to change this. They will still have the Right to Buy, but tenants who take up lettings after the transfer will not have the Right to Buy. The level of rights will depend on the terms agreed with the new landlord, which will depend to a certain degree on Housing Corporation guidance — the "Tenants' Guarantee" (published in January 1989) for registered housing associations; and Appendix 2 to the big orange booklet — "Tenants' Choice: Criteria for Landlord Approval and Guidance Notes for Applicants" (published in January 1989), for bodies which are not registered housing associations. There may be a further guidance document for fully mutual co-operatives.

The Housing Corporation publication — "Advice on Tenancy Terms" (May 1989) — spells out the differences between secure tenancies and tenancies available through the Change of Landlord scheme.

One point to note here is that the assured tenancy possession Ground 6 (redevelopment) cannot be used, because transfer from secure tenancy to assured tenancy status does not amount to a new tenancy as such (it is merely an agreement to a change in tenancy terms). Therefore the precondition for use of Ground 6, that the landlord has to have owned the property since before the tenancy began, cannot be met.

The key point about the status of this guidance is that if a landlord body reneges on it then the level of rights the tenant will actually have will ultimately be decided by the courts — on the basis of the Housing Act 1988 rules for assured tenancies — and they provide far fewer rights than those which secure tenants have enjoyed under the Tenants' Charter which arose out of the 1980 Housing Act.

If the landlord reneges, the options are:

a) the tenants take individual action for breach of contract,
b) the tenants persuade the Housing Corporation to help them take a breach of contract action,
c) the Housing Corporation itself takes a breach of contract action concerning its contract with the landlord (see earlier in this Guide, at 4.2, for details of this "Deed under Seal"),
d) the Housing Corporation takes action under the revocation procedure (although this will not help existing tenants), or
e) the Housing Corporation takes action against a registered housing association under its general powers.

If the landlord and tenant contract for better terms than are contained in the Act, e.g. the landlord will not utilise a particular Ground for possession, then if the landlord breaches the terms of the contract the tenant's only hope of proper redress is to challenge the breach of contract before the landlord seeks to use the Act's provision in the county court. If the tenant challenges the landlord's breach of contract in court (e.g. after receiving a NOSP), the court may grant an injunction to stop the breach. But if the tenant does nothing, and the landlord does seek to use a provision of the Act which is not included in the contract, then the court is likely to follow the statute – not the contract.

b. Rents.

In spite of the requirement in the "Tenants' Choice" criteria that rents of transferred tenanted accommodation should remain within the reach of people in low paid employment rents are bound to increase, because they will be set according to market forces. The rents charged, and future rent increases, will in large part depend on how much the new landlord pays the council for the housing taken over (in some cases the council may have to pay the new landlord), and how much the new landlord will need in order to carry out repairs. This said, the issue will undoubtedly be clouded by Government attempts, primarily through the 1989 Local Government and Housing legislation, to force councils to raise their own rents substantially, as a means of reducing the willingness of tenants to stay with their present landlord.

As for rents payable following lease-back, local authorities will be charged the average new rents as charged on assured tenancies of the transferred properties, but they will have to make the difficult decision whether or not to pass on the full higher rent payable under "Tenants' Choice" guidance, or to retain the existing public sector rent. If they choose the latter they will then have to make the other council tenants subsidise that rent.

c. Service charges.

Although transfered tenants' rents are meant to be affordable to people in low-paid employment (see the "Tenants' Choice" criteria) there is no similar rule concerning service charges.

Where a new landlord takes over the freehold when a tenant of a flat has opted to stay with the local authority, the local authority will become liable for any service charges made by the freeholder. The authority will then be free to decide whether or not to pass them on to the tenant.

d. Succession.

Succession rights of tenants who stay with the council.

Where there has been a vote under the "Tenants' Choice" proposals, and a secure tenant under the Housing Act 1985 has opted to remain with a local authority, rather than opt for a new landlord, existing succession rights will be kept. These are the right of a spouse to succeed to the Housing Act 1985 secure tenancy, and the right of a non-spouse relative to succeed to the secure tenancy, as long as the relative has lived in the accommodation for the last year of the tenant's life. Only one succession is allowed. It is important to note that where flats are concerned, if the successor dies (whether spouse or other relative) the property passes out of the control of the local authority. This is because even though the "Tenants' Choice" decision went against the proposed new landlord the freehold passed to that body, and the local authority only kept control through a leasing arrangement for as long as the tenant or a successor remained as tenants. So on the death of a successor the new landlord has control, and can relet or sell the property. This will not apply with houses because where the tenant has opted to stay with the local authority landlord the authority retains the freehold.

e. Succession rights of tenants who opt for a new landlord

Rights will depend on the Housing Corporation guidance already mentioned, and on negotiation, but as with other rights ultimately it is the 1988 Housing Act rules which will decide, if a landlord decided to renege on its pledges. Under the Act spouses have a right to succeed, but other relatives do not. See Part 1 of this Guide for details. (See also our paragraph 5.5F in relation to the preserved Right to Buy where a family member takes over a tenancy).

Negotiated terms will be binding under contract law, even if the terms involve more rights than are to be found in the Act. A tenant would be able to seek legal remedies following any breach of the contract terms by the landlord.

4.8 DISPOSAL OF ACCOMMODATION BY THE NEW LANDLORD

A LANDLORD WHO HAS OBTAINED accommodation under the Change of Landlord part of the Act cannot dispose of it without the Secretary of State's consent. But no consent will be needed for:

- tenants to exercise their Right to Buy (which they will retain), but this only applies to the original transferring tenants.
- leases-back to the landlord.
- compulsory disposals under Part V of the 1985 Housing Act.
- a number of other "technical" disposals, such as the grant of a legal charge to secure a loan, and the grant of an assured tenancy.

Disposals to housing associations will be the subject of consultations with the Housing Corporation.

In a written reply to a Parliamentary Question, Junior Environment Minister David Trippier said, on March 22nd 1989 (Hansard, Cols. 649 and 650):

"We understand that some prospective acquirers of property under these powers have it in mind to apply, at the time when a mortgage or other charge is granted on transferred property as security for a loan, for my consent to subsequent disposals should certain defined circumstances arise. My right hon. Friend shall, of course, consider all applications for consent under sections 105 and 133 . . . (of the 1988 Housing Act) . . . on their merits. Subject to that, however, my right hon. Friend shall be prepared in principle to consider sympathetically applications at the time when such mortgages and charges are to be granted, for my consent under either section 105 or section 133 to subsequent disposals of transferred dwellings by named mortgagees and chargees in the exercise of a power of sale, provided: that the dwellings to be disposed of are vacant when the power of sale is exercised; that the sales are to individuals intending to use the dwellings as their only or principal homes; that the sales are at the best price that can reasonably be obtained; and that the sales are by the mortgagee or chargee in exercise of the power of sale contained in the original mortgage or charge."

A landlord who makes an application to the Secretary of State must have consulted the tenants in that property. The Secretary of State must — "have regard" — to the tenants' response. In exercising this discretion the Secretary of State has to bear in mind the undertaking which applicant landlord bodies entered into as a condition of their approval — "to retain dwellings acquired as a Tenants' Choice landlord for letting at rents within reach of those in low-paid employment".

Where a property has been leased-back the new landlord can dispose of it in the same way as property which has been transferred to them directly (as long as the lease has been ended properly), and the leased-back tenants must be consulted in the same way as ordinary tenants of the new landlord.

5. Other issues

INTRODUCTION

PART V of the Act covers a wide range of issues. These include an extra task for Rent Officers, who will have to check the rents of tenants who apply for housing benefit. The aim is to reduce the rent allowance subsidy local authorities receive from central government. If the Rent Officer considers the rent to be unreasonably high, the local authority will only receive subsidy up to the level of rent the Rent Officer considers reasonable, although the local authority can still choose to pay housing benefit on the basis of the higher rent. Other aspects of Part V include changes concerning the Right to Buy; transferrable discounts; repair notices and obligations; local authority voluntary disposal of housing; and the enabling power for a Commission for Racial Equality Housing Code of Practice to be issued.

5.1 PREMIUMS ON LONG LEASES

THIS PROVISION (SECTION 115) came into force on January 15th 1989.

Premiums will be chargeable on long leases as long as the landlord has no power to end the tenancy within 20 years of its start (except for breach of tenancy terms), and the tenancy terms do not inhibit assignment and sub-letting of the whole of the accommodation (except during the last seven years of the lease).

5.2 TENANCIES EXCLUDED FROM BANKRUPT'S ESTATE

THESE PROVISIONS (SECTIONS 117 AND 118) came into force on January 15th 1989.

The Insolvency Act 1986, and the Bankruptcy (Scotland) Act 1985, are amended to exclude categories of protected and assured tenancies, with no financial value, from being vested in the trustee to a bankruptcy. But where there is a value, e.g. an assured tenancy that can be assigned because it is subject to a premium, vesting will still take place as such a tenancy is a potential asset to the creditors of a bankrupt's estate.

5.3 LANDLORD AND TENANT ACT 1987

THIS PROVISION (SECTION 119), which deals with loopholes in the 1987 Act, came into force on January 15th 1989. Leaseholders of flats which include common parts are given the right of first refusal where the landlord wants to sell, and the right to have defects in their leases corrected, and the right in certain circumstances to compulsorily purchase the freehold.

But note that it is subject to transitional provisions set out in SI 1988 No. 2152. These say that:- "the amendments to the Landlord and Tenant Act 1987 in paragraphs 1, 2(2) and 3 of Schedule 13 to the Housing Act 1988 do not have effect in relation to a disposal (within the meaning of Part I of that Act) made in pursuance of a contract entered into before January 15th 1989 or made under that Act where the offer notice was served, or treated as served, under section 5 of the 1987 Act before that date."

The transitional provisions also say — "The amendments to the 1987 Act in paragraphs 4 to 6 of that Schedule do not apply in relation to an application made to the court before the 15th January 1989."

Note that 1988 Housing Act assured tenants do not have a right of first refusal where the landlord intends to sell the accommodation.

5.4 RENT OFFICERS INVOLVEMENT IN HOUSING BENEFIT

THESE PROVISIONS (SECTIONS 120 AND 121) came into force on January 15th 1989.

A. APPOINTMENT OF RENT OFFICERS

The Act gives the Secretary of State powers to amalgamate rent officer registration areas, for reasons of insufficient work or more efficient administration — following consultation with local authorities; and to take away the appointment, remuneration and administration of rent officers from local authorities.

B. RENT OFFICERS AND HOUSING BENEFIT

Although rent officers will continue to have a role in setting the maximum rents that can be charged by landlords of tenancies regulated under the 1977 Rent Act, the 1988 Housing Act opens the way for them to have a separate and additional role. It gives the Secretary of State power to require rent officers to carry out functions concerning housing benefit and rent allowance subsidy.

Note that the arrangements set out below do not apply to tenancies which began before January 15th 1989 (January 2nd 1989 in Scotland). In their case local authorities will not refer housing benefit applications to a Rent Officer for assessment. Instead the pre−1988 Housing Act system of local rent thresholds apply, with the local authority receiving only 25% housing benefit subsidy (instead of the normal 97%) on any part of the rent which is above that threshold. In such cases if it pays housing benefit on the rent above the threshold it will have to take the money from its General Rate Fund.

From 1st April 1989, where there is a claim for housing benefit, for all lettings from January 15th 1989 (except new lets to Rent Act regulated tenants, by the same landlord) local authorities will have to refer housing benefit applications to the Rent Officer, who will have to decide whether the rent payable by the tenant is reasonable for the purposes of housing benefit subsidy; and whether the accommodation is "over-large" for the claimant's "reasonable needs". The Rent Officer will assess a "reasonable market rent", but the rent assessed will relate to the issue of housing benefit subsidy — not what the landlord can charge, nor what level of housing benefit the local authority can pay. Housing benefit application forms will ask applicants for more information than was previously required.

There is a transitional arrangement. New lettings made between January 15th 1989 (January 2nd 1989 in Scotland), and April 4th 1989 will be referred to the Rent Officer from April 17th 1989 on a gradual basis as housing benefit claims fall due for review.

The new role of Rent Officers, and the effect on housing benefit claims, is bound to be complex and confusing. In theory there is a separation between the Rent Officers' role in assessing rents for subsidy purposes, and the local authorities' role of restricting housing benefit by applying rent stops. However, the new regulations do entitle local authorities to have regard to Rent Officer determinations when restricting payments of housing benefit under Regulations 11 and 12. There are therefore bound to be numerous cases where authorities automatically restrict the eligible rent to the amount considered reasonable by the Rent Officer, and advisers will find this even more difficult to challenge than in the past.

What the landlord can charge will be determined by the Rent Act 1977 (for tenancies protected under that Act — most being pre-1988 Housing Act lettings); and by the 1988 Housing Act (for assured, and assured shorthold tenancies).

Rents determined by Rent Assessment Committees for assured and assured shorthold lettings under the 1988 Housing Act will automatically be accepted as reasonable for housing benefit subsidy purposes, but the housing benefit claim will still be referred to the Rent Officer to consider whether the accommodation is "overlarge".

The detail of the scheme is set out in SI No. 590 — The Rent Officers (Additional Functions) Order 1989 — which came into force on April 1st 1989. It was subject to the approval of both the Commons and the Lords. But any SI introduced in future to vary the arrangements will pass automatically unless specifically opposed in either House.

The arrangements are amplified by DSS Circulars HB(88)17, and HB(89)6, issued in November 1988 and March 1989 respectively. Both are called "Housing Benefit Subsidy — Rent Officer Referral Arrangements".

The essence of the scheme is that from April 1st 1989, applications to local authorities for housing benefit for all private rented lettings beginning on or after January 15th 1989 (January 2nd in Scotland) will be referred to Rent Officers. This includes boarders not housed as such under the homelessness legislation. It excludes new Rent Act regulated tenancies allowed by Section 34 of the 1988 Housing Act.

● If a claimant refuses to let a Rent Officer enter the accommodation, the local authority can withhold payment of housing benefit.
● Under Housing Benefit Regulation 88, local authorities must pay housing benefit within 14 days, or as soon as possible afterwards. Rent Officers should tell local authorities of their decision within 5 working days. If longer than 5 days the Rent Officer will make an interim determination.
● The local authority can appeal against a Rent Officer's decision, within 10 days of the decision. The claimant has no appeal.

5.5 RIGHT TO BUY

5.5A VARIATION OF THE COST FLOOR FOR DISCOUNT

This provision came into force on March 10th 1989.

Before the Act the Right to Buy discount was not allowed to push the purchase price below the cost, since 31st March 1974, of building or improving the property. The Government's original intention was to abolish this limit, called the "cost floor". But the Act merely modifies it to an eight year rolling period. So the relevent year for discounts in 1989 would be 1981, and so on. The Act gives the Secretary of State power to make an Order to vary the time period.

5.5B DISABLED PERSONS

This provision (Section 123) came into force on January 15th 1989.

Through repeal of paragraphs 6 and 8 of Schedule 5 to the Housing Act 1985, housing which is purpose built, converted, or adapted for people with physical disabilities is no longer exempt from the Right to Buy — unless it is part of a sheltered scheme, i.e. where a group of properties has been specially designed or adapted, and special facilities are provided nearby by the Social Services Department.

Note that housing provided for people with mental illness, or for elderly people, is still excepted from the Right to Buy.

5.5C TENANT'S SANCTION FOR LANDLORD'S DELAYS

This provision (Section 124) came into force on March 10th 1989. It adds Sections 153A and 153B to Part V of the Housing Act 1985.

If the landlord fails to meet the Right to Buy deadlines imposed by sections 124, 125, 146 and 147 of the Housing Act 1985, secure tenants can apply (via a Notice of Delay) to have their rent deducted from the purchase price. If the delay is for more than a year compensation will be one and a half times the rent.

A further provision came into force on March 10th 1989. Schedule 17, Paragraph 41, of the 1988 Housing Act — which amends section 155 of the Housing Act 1985. It relates to Notice of Delay, and defines relevant dates. SI 240 — The Housing (Right to Buy Delay Procedure)(Prescribed Forms) Regulations 1989 — came into force on March 10th 1989. These Regulations prescribe the notices to be served on or by a landlord under Sections 153A and 153B of the Housing Act 1985.

5.5D RESTRICTION ON LETTING IN NATIONAL PARKS ETC.

This provision (Section 125) came into force on January 15th 1989.

When public landlords sell homes voluntarily — in National Parks; areas of outstanding natural beauty; and designated rural areas under section 157 of the Housing Act 1985 — the Act enables them to impose a restrictive covenant concerning future letting. It does so by amending section 37 of the Housing Act 1985.

The restrictive covenant can require the purchaser who wishes to let to someone else (on a tenancy or a licence), to only do so to someone who either had his/her place of work, or only home in the area. Letting to anyone else can only take place with the local authority's consent.

5.5E RESTRICTION ON LETTINGS IN NATIONAL PARKS ETC., WHERE THE ACCOMMODATION HAS BEEN ACQUIRED UNDER THE RIGHT TO BUY

This provision (Section 126) came into force on January 15th 1989.

The Act amends section 157 of the Housing Act 1985 to allow a local authority to impose the same kind of restricted covenant where the accommodation has been acquired under the right to buy in the three classes of area already noted.

5.5F PRESERVED RIGHT TO BUY

This provision (Section 127) came into force on April 5th 1989.

Under Section 127, if a secure tenant becomes an assured tenant, with the preserved Right to Buy, a family member who takes over the tenancy under the will or intestacy on the tenant's death also has the Right to Buy, and if s/he assigns the tenancy to another family member that person will have it too.

If a tenant with the preserved Right to Buy becomes the tenant of a housing association while still in that property, the Right to Buy will be retained (unless it is a charitable housing trust, and a "conflict with the trusts of the charity" would arise.)

SI 368 — The Housing (Preservation of Right to Buy) Regulations 1989 — came into force on April 5th 1989. They modify Part V of the 1985 Housing Act concerning where an authority which is the landlord of a secure tenant disposes of the accommodation but where the Right to Buy is preserved. The three main changes are — no right to a mortgage; no right to claim a shared ownership lease; and the preserved right to buy will be exercisable against certain housing associations (broadly, charities and ones which have not received Government or local authority grants) which are excepted from the main Right to Buy.

5.5G RIGHT TO BUY DISCOUNTS

Four Statutory Instruments concerning Right to Buy discounts came into force in the first half of 1989. They are as follows:-

SI 174 — The Housing (Right to Buy)(Prescribed Persons) Order 1989 — came into force on March 10th 1989. It adds 5 bodies (including the Church Commissioners) to the list of bodies which count as public sector landlords so that people who were previously their tenants are able to count that time towards discount.

SI 239 — The Housing (Right to Buy)(Prescribed Forms)(Amendment) Regulations 1989 — came into force on March 10th 1989. This makes minor changes to the notice claiming the Right to Buy, and also says that Housing Action Trusts count as public sector landlords for the purpose of tenancy time counting towards discount — as under SI 174 above.

SI 512 — The Housing (Preservation of Right to Buy)(Amendment) Regulations 1989 — came into force on April 5th 1989. Where someone exercises the preserved Right to Buy, the price payable is reduced by an amount of discount calculated according to Sections 129 to 131 and Schedule 4 of the 1985 Housing Act. These Regulations amend Section 131 to increase the maximum discount from £35,000 to £50,000.

SI 513 — The Housing (Right to Buy)(Maximum Discount) Order 1989 — came into force on April 11th 1989. It simply increases the maximum discount under the Right to Buy itself, from £35,000 to £50,000.

5.6 TRANSFERABLE DISCOUNTS

THIS PROVISION CAME INTO FORCE on April 1st 1989. It gives local authorities a specific statutory power to give money to their tenants to buy private accommodation, so that they cease to be council tenants or licensees. Each scheme is subject to the Secretary of State's approval.

The money can be:-
a) to buy accommodation; or
b) to carry out works to a dwelling to provide additional accommodation; or
c) both a) and b).

Although local authorities appear to have been given a lot of discretion concerning these schemes, it is clear that the Secretary of State has retained considerable powers concerning the conditions of approval, publicity, revocation, and grant.

Grants made under these schemes will be regarded as capital expenditure, and will be debited to the Housing Revenue Account.

5.7 REPAIR NOTICES

THIS PROVISION (SECTION 130) came into force on January 15th 1989.

These powers can be used against private landlords and housing associations.

Section 130 and Schedule 15 of the Act give local councils wider duties to serve and enforce repair notices, under Part VI of the Housing Act 1985, where properties are unfit, and stronger powers where they are in serious disrepair. The new powers include — a new offence where the landlord fails to comply with a repairs notice; the power to serve a notice on the landlord even if the tenant has not asked the council to do so; making sure the landlord cannot avoid the notices by hiding behind a 'front' company; stronger powers to carry out works itself if the landlord fails to do so (and making it easier for the council to recoup the costs from the landlord); power to serve repairs notices on blocks of flats; and higher fines.

NOTE: It is an applied term of assured tenancies that the tenant will give the landlord reasonable access to carry out repairs.

5.8 REPAIRING OBLIGATIONS IN SHORT LEASES

THIS PROVISION (SECTION 116) came into force on January 15th 1989.

Section 116 of the Act amends Section 11 of the Landlord and Tenant Act 1985 to extend landlords' repairing obligations in short leases (i.e. leases which are granted for less than 7 years. Weekly, fortnightly, and monthly tenancies are among those which fall into this category.)

The amendment extends the landlords' obligations to installations used in common by more than one tenant. This extension only applies to leases beginning on or after January 15th 1989. And it does not apply to licences or Crown lettings. Housing Action Trusts are added to the list of bodies excluded from section 11 obligations. This puts them on a par with local authorities concerning use of short-life property.

5.9 LETTING CONDITIONS REGARDING IMPROVEMENT GRANTS

THIS PROVISION (SECTION 131) came into force on January 15th 1989.

Changes are made to Part XV of the Housing Act 1985, as a result of the introduction of new forms of letting under this Act.

Firstly, under the pre-1988 Housing Act rules, in order to get a grant a landlord had to show intention to live there him/herself or to let the accommodation for a minimum 5 years after the works had been carried out. These requirements do not change, but the Act blocks a loophole. This occurred where the landlord grants a long-lease (i.e. 21 years or over) and claims that in doing so the "certificate of availability for letting" requirements have been met.

Secondly, the Section also enables the local authority to impose as a condition of the grant that the premises will be let on an assured tenancy which is not a long-lease.

5.10 VOLUNTARY DISPOSALS OF HOUSING STOCK

GOVERNMENT POLICY ON voluntary transfers is set out not only in this Act but also in a DoE paper published in June 1988 — "Large Scale Voluntary Disposals of Local Authority Housing to Private Bodies."

At the time of writing (May 1989) tenants had voted in favour of voluntary transfer schemes covering four local authorities — Sevenoaks, Chiltern, Broadlands and Newbury. Tenants had voted against schemes in Arun, Torbay, Rochford, Salisbury, Gloucester and Three Rivers. The Secretary of State's consent to the disposals in Sevenoaks and Chilterns had been given and they had taken place.

The position of charitable housing associations concerning the acquisition of tenanted housing under voluntary transfers has been covered earlier in this Guide (see 2.20).

Nothing in this Act prevents a local authority voluntarily disposing of its housing stock after the Change of Landlord part of the Act came into force on April 5th 1989. The Secretary of State has said he hopes that the Change of Landlord voting system will be used for voluntary transfer schemes after April 1989.

The question of what happens if an outside landlord body intends to make a bid for part of the housing stock at the same time as the present landlord is trying to transfer all its stock to another body, was answered by a joint statement (April 5th 1989) from the Department of the Environment and the Housing Corporation — "Arrangements for Interaction Between Tenants' Choice and other powers for Transferring Public Sector Housing." This statement sets out the principle that — ". . . only one transfer proposal . . . should be able to proceed at any one time, and must be allowed to run its course before another transfer proposal affecting some or all of the same dwellings can be set in train." This does however beg the question of what is meant by "running its course".

The rules for tenant consultation under "Voluntary Transfer" are set out in Circular 6/88 — "Consultation with Secure Tenants before Disposal to Private Sector Landlords: Commencement of Section 6 of the Housing and Planning Act 1986" — which adds Section 106A, and Schedule 3A to the 1985 Housing Act. The Secretary of State's consent has to be obtained before a "Voluntary Transfer" can go ahead. The Schedule says that if he is dissatisfied with the consultation, he can order further consultations; and if he thinks that a majority of the tenants affected do not wish the transfer to take place he must not give his consent. In practice this means that consultation will be undertaken by way of a ballot, even though there is nothing in the legislation to say one has to be held. Unlike "Tenants' Choice" there is no lease-back option for those who object to it if the transfer goes ahead.

Where there are rent arrears prior to a transfer the general principle which would seem to apply is that the new landlord starts off with no past liabilities. This means in effect that the old landlord would have to pursue pre-transfer arrears as a civil debt.

5.10A CONSENTS FOR DISPOSALS AND USE OF RECEIPTS

Section 132 (which came into force, retrospectively, on June 9th 1988) says that in giving consent to a disposal (and in deciding any conditions to be attached to consent) under the Housing Act 1985 the Secretary of State "may" have regard to:-

a) the extent to which the intending purchaser "is, or is likely to be, dependent upon, controlled by or subject to influence from the local authority making the disposal or any members or officers of that authority";

b) the extent to which the disposal would result in the purchaser becoming

"the predominant or a substantial owner in any area of housing accommodation let on tenancies or subject to licences";
c) the terms of the disposal; and
d) "any other matters whatsoever which he considers relevant."

5.10B CONSENT FOR CERTAIN SUBSEQUENT DISPOSALS

This provision (Section 133) came into force on November 15th 1988.

This Section applies to voluntary transfers only. Rules for subsequent disposals for "Tenants' Choice" have been explained earlier in this Guide (see 4.8). Where a landlord has acquired the property under a procedure where consent was required (under sections 32 or 43 of the Housing Act 1985) and "that consent does not provide otherwise" the person who acquired it cannot dispose of it to someone else without the Secretary of State's consent.

The Secretary of State must not give consent unless he is satisfied that "appropriate steps" have been taken to consult "every tenant of any land or house proposed to be disposed of", and unless he has "had regard to the responses of any such tenants to that consultation". But no ground rules are laid down for these responsibilities.

5.10C CAPITAL RECEIPTS AND DISPOSAL COSTS

This provision (Section 136) came into force on January 15th 1989.

This section amends section 430 of the Housing Act 1985, to enable capital receipts to be used to pay the administrative costs of voluntary disposals.

5.10D PRESERVED RIGHT TO BUY

Although not stemming directly from the 1988 Housing Act it should be noted that SI 1989 No. 430 brought into force, on April 5th 1989, Section 8 of the 1986 Housing and Planning Act. Section 8 provides for the provisions of Part V of the 1985 Housing Act (the right to buy) to continue to apply where a person ceases to be a secure tenant of a dwelling-house because the landlord has disposed of an interest in that dwelling-house to a private sector landlord.

5.11 RACE RELATIONS — CRE CODES OF PRACTICE

THIS PROVISION (SECTION 137) came into force on January 15th 1989.

The Act enables the Commission for Racial Equality to produce a Code of Practice, to apply to all leased, rented, or licenced housing. In March 1989 the CRE published a consultation draft of its proposed Code:- "Race Relations Code of Practice for the elimination of racial discrimination and the promotion of equal opportunity in the field of rented housing."

The Code will be supplemented by detailed advisory guides on good practice on race and housing issues, including guides on training, positive action and ethnic monitoring. The Government amended the Local Government and Housing Bill to extend the CRE's code-making powers to the remaining areas of housing, for example estate agencies and lending institutions. There will be consultation on this after the Bill has become law.

The Code (which lists many illustrative examples of discrimination) will provide detailed guidance on the operation of the 1976 Race Relations Act in relation to rented housing and the elimination of racial discrimination — and to give examples of good practice in the implementation and promotion of equal opportunities. It will cover — "the social rented sector, which includes local authorities, the voluntary sector (housing associations and cooperatives), Tenants' Choice Landlords and Housing Action Trusts; and the private rented sector, which includes private landlords, landladies and accommodation agencies, the functions of estate agents where they relate to the letting of accommodation, hotel and hostel accommodation, and services provided by the local authority."

In the words of the draft Code, "The Code does not impose any legal obligations itself, nor is it an authoritative statement of the law — this can only be provided by the courts and tribunals. If, however, its recommendations are not observed, this may result in breaches of the law where an act or omission falls within any of the specific prohibitions of the Act."

Moreover, the Code's provisions are admissible in evidence in any proceedings under the Race Relations Act before the courts, and if any provision appears to be relevant to a question arising in the proceedings, it must be taken into account in determining that question.

Some of the key points made in the draft Code are as follows:-

● As housing organisations are employers as well as service providers the housing Code should be read in conjunction with the CRE's employment Code — as achieving equal opportunity in housing cannot be separated from equal opportunity in employment.

● All landlords and other housing bodies should:

+ review systematically all their policies on a regular basis;

+ implement an equal opportunity policy, including local authority services such as the rent officer, tenancy relations, and legal services — backed by staff training, translated documents and interpretation services. A staff training programme should be set up — and cover ability to implement and monitor the equal opportunity policy, full awareness of the implications of the 1976 Race Relations Act, review of policies and practices, effective ethnic record keeping and monitoring, and effective policies to counter racial harassment;

+ review their allocation systems and base them on clear criteria;

+ set up ethnic record keeping and monitoring systems concerning access to housing, the quality of housing offered, and service delivery. Analytical monitoring reports should be produced at least every six months, and made available to tenants and local people. Problems identified should be timetabled for rectification;

+ identify the particular needs of ethnic minorities in any given area — e.g. building programmes — and then devising appropriate strategies. To ensure equal treatment for different ethnic groups a measurement, or target, should be agreed, of the proportions of ethnic minorities that could be expected if equal opportunity was being achieved — but these should not be confused with predetermined quotas, unlawful under the Race Relations Act;

+ ensure that information is readily available to local communities and translated into the relevant languages;

+ adopt specific measures for particular groups to enable them to overcome communication difficulties — e.g. translation;

+ ensure that staff do not base subjective assessments on racial origin;

+ develop a policy for dealing with discriminatory instructions from landlords and landladies, hostels, and hotel owners or managers — particularly concerning accommodation agencies and local authority housing advisory services — including notification of the CRE, discontinued use of the hostel etc., and notification of other agencies;

+ accommodation agencies (including universities and housing advice centres) should adopt a monitoring procedure to safeguard against discrimination — based on random checks of agencies' records of vacant accommodation and landlords; occasional random checks to ensure applicants have been given details of all appropriate vacancies available; and accommodation bureaux for institutional lettings should prepare a six monthly report on equal opportunity policy implementation and the results of such checks;

+ not ask for passports as a matter of routine when identification is required;

+ adopt a comprehensive strategy to counter racial harassment, including:

– clear guidelines for staff on what action they should take in cases of racial harassment, and effective monitoring;

– an effective support system for victims, set up by larger landlords, with efficient rehousing arrangements available, and close monitoring where tenants wish to stay in their homes. Smaller landlords should assist victims, and contact the police, local authority, local CRC etc.;

– landlords should try to identify the perpetrators of racial attacks and take appropriate action – including contacting the police and, if all the circumstances justify it, seeking a court order for possession. Racial harassment should be included in tenancy agreements as grounds for terminating the agreement;

– tenants and prospective tenants on waiting lists should be advised that racial harassment will not be tolerated and action will be taken when incidents occur. Policies should be adopted to deal with racist graffiti;

– larger landlords should set up an effective and regular system of liaison with other agencies – e.g. community groups, the police and the local authority. Common strategies should be developed between various large landlords (e.g. local authorities, housing associations, HATs). Landlords should strive for the support and agreement of tenants associations and other representative groups for a common front on tackling racial harassment;

– local authorities should promote a strategy for the prevention of racial harassment, and to assist the process of dealing with cases in the private sector;

– larger housing organisations in particular should take advantage of the positive action provisions of the Race Relations Act. This includes, among others, designated training bodies and employers encouraging applications from (or making training facilities available to) persons of a particular racial group, where there is under-representation, although this does not allow discrimination in favour of persons of that group in making appointments. There is a CRE booklet — "Positive Action and Equal Opportunities in Employment." A CRE booklet on positive action in housing will be published in 1989.

The Government has given a clear commitment to extend the power to make such a Code to all forms of tenure at the earliest legislative opportunity.

5.12 CONSEQUENTIAL ISSUES

SECTIONS 138 (CONSEQUENTIAL FINANCIAL PROVISIONS); 139 (Application of the Act to the Isles of Scilly); and 141 (Short title, commencement and extent of the Act) all came into force on November 15th 1988.

SI 1988 No. 2152, and SI 1989 No. 404, relate to a complex weave of dates on which minor and consequential amendments to previous legislation, and repeals, came into force. In large part these relate to Section 140. In a number of cases amendments and repeals are subject to special provisions. These too are set out in these Statutory Instruments.

The 1988 Housing Act does not extend to Northern Ireland. Parts I (Private Renting); III ((HATs); and IV (Change of Landlord); and V (Miscellaneous and General) except Sections 118, 128, 132, 134, 135, 137, 139, 140 and 141, England and Wales only.

6. Conclusions

This Act has to be seen as only a part of the Government's legislative campaign to privatise housing. The next legislative initiative is the Housing and Local Government Bill, which will prevent local authorities subsidising their tenants' rents from the rates. It is aimed at forcing rents up high enough so that council tenants think twice before voting to stay with the council, under the Change of Landlord proposals in this Act, or under voluntary transfer initiatives.

In our view the shift of emphasis under the 1988 Housing Act, towards private provision of rented housing, and away from public provision, will result in a continuing decline of rented housing, not an increased supply. The planning of housing provision will be marginalised, and new housing of an adequate standard will appear only where potential occupants are able to afford it. In most cases the cost will make owner-occupation a more attractive option. But for the huge numbers of people who cannot afford either option the future will be bleak.

The Act will further undermine the capacities of local authorities and housing associations to plan and supply the accommodation needed by low income households.
For many people the Act will mean fewer opportunities for access to a home; ineffective rights for those lucky enough to get a home; and a considerable increase in the incidence of eviction — both legal and illegal. And turning the full circle, people made homeless will find it all the more difficult to find a decent, secure, affordable home.

The wedge between the two-thirds of our society who are well-off, and the one-third who are not, will be driven in even harder by the 1988 Housing Act. Poorer communities will be displaced by those with financial power. Housing options will be increasingly closed.

Sadly, the 1988 Housing Act represents a theory, not a policy. There is a policy vacuum. SHELTER believes that housing policy should be based on clear criteria, which reflect the basic demand for housing. In our view the key criteria are:-
● genuinely affordable homes, with the cost to the consumer being set at a

level which minimises the **need** for assistance with housing costs as far as possible;
● security of tenure;
● good quality accommodation, properly maintained;
● letting based on need, not wealth;
● access based on equal opportunity;
● the occupant having a say over the management of the property.

This Act is a move in the opposite direction.

Appendix one:
Glossary of terms

assured tenure
Assured tenancies were originally introduced by the 1980 Housing Act. The 1988 Housing Act assured tenancy regime is unrelated to that of the 1980 Housing Act regime. Private landlords and housing associations can use them without the safeguards of the original scheme. Market rents will apply. In limited circumstances the Rent Assessment Committee will be able to set a rent — its version of a market rent. To evict a tenant the landlord will have to go to the county court on the basis of one or more Grounds for possession.

assured shorthold tenure
Assured shorthold tenure is a category within the 1988 Housing Act assured tenure regime. Assured shortholds are fixed-term tenancies of 6 months or more. Market rents apply, and during the initial fixed-term the tenant can apply to the Rent Assessment Committee for its version of a market rent. After the fixed-term the landlord can at any time apply to the county court for possession, as long as 2 months notice has been given to the tenant.

regulated, contractual, protected and statutory tenancies
Regulated tenancies are those which have the full protection of the 1977 Rent Act. Contractual or protected tenancies are those where a contract (oral or written) is still in force between the landlord and the tenant. When a contractual or protected tenancy comes to an end the tenant is still protected by the 1977 Rent Act (statute) — and therefore becomes a statutory tenant.

restricted contracts
Lettings under the Rent Act 1977 where the landlord lives in the same building as the occupant (except a purpose built block of flats); or where the rent includes insubstantial board (i.e. food), or substantial attendances (e.g. personal services such as cleaning of rooms). People in this position are called restricted contract tenants or licensees.

long leases, short leases
Long leases are where the tenancy is granted for more than 21 years at a rent which is less than two-thirds the rateable value of the property. **Short leases** are where the tenancy is granted for less than 7 years. They include the general type of tenancies held — e.g. weekly, fortnightly, monthly.

assignment
The transfer of an interest in a property to another person or body. The rules

governing assignment vary according to the tenure status of the occupier.

"fair" rents
Regulated tenants have the right to apply to the Rent Officer to have a fair rent set and registered for their accommodation. The Rent Officer has to ignore scarcity value (i.e. the value added on by demand outstripping supply).

"reasonable" rents
Restricted contract holders have the right to apply to the Rent Tribunal for a reasonable rent to be set and registered.

market rents
Generally, a market rent will be what the landlord chooses to charge. However, where the rent of an assured or an assured shorthold tenancy is referred to a Rent Assessment Committee, the Committee will determine its version of a market rent — although at the time of writing no Government guidance had been given to them on how to do it. Rents for assured and assured shorthold housing association tenancies, which under the Act can be market rents, will be somewhat less because of the substantial element of Housing Association Grant public funding which associations will receive.

rent assessment committee
Rents set by the rent officer can be referred to the Rent Assessment Committee for review. Under the 1988 Housing Act the Rent Assessment Committee has an additional function — to set a market rent (on application) for assured and assured shorthold tenancies.

housing association grant (HAG)
Every year the Government sets the overall funding limit for the Housing Corporation (the body which governs housing associations' activities). The Housing Corporation then sets the Approved Development Programme (ADP), and follows this with the level of public grant which is to fund that programme. Before the 1988 Housing Act HAG was generally around 100%. The 1988 Housing Act does not set different limits, as legislation is not needed to do so. On December 14th 1988 the Housing Corporation announced an average HAG of 75%.

housing action trusts
Housing Action Trusts (HATs) are non-elected bodies set up by the Government to take over and become the new landlord of an area of mainly local authority housing (e.g. an estate) and land; and then improve the housing and the environment. They will each have about a 5 year life. They will then wind up and the housing will be passed on to other landlords. They are not

elected bodies. They will take over many of the functions of the local authority, but not its homelessness duties.

negative valuation (or dowry)
Under the HATs scheme introduced by Part III of the Act; under the change of landlord scheme introduced by Part IV of the Act; and under voluntary transfers of estates enabled by the 1986 Housing and Planning Act — in cases where the properties involved are in very poor condition the local authority may well have to pay the landlord body which is taking over. This would be a negative valuation, and is often referred to as a "dowry".

SI (statutory instrument, or order)
There has been a growing trend in recent years for Governments to use Acts of Parliament to introduce a general framework of a policy, and to give wide powers to Secretaries of State to legislate the substance by statutory instrument — also called an Order. Governments like them because they weaken MPs' and Peers' ability to interfere with them. For example, they can only be passed as a whole or rejected as a whole — they cannot be amended. Statutory instruments fall into various categories. Some, for example those which simply enact dates when parts of an Act come into force, are simply nodded through Parliament. On more substantive issues there are two types — those subject to the affirmative procedure, and those subject to the negative procedure. Affirmative orders do not pass unless both Houses of Parliament actively approve them. Negative orders pass automatically unless they are objected to in the Commons — in which case they are debated. It is very rare indeed for a statutory instrument to be defeated, and they are usually timetabled very late at night or at other awkward times when few parliamentarians are present.

Appendix two: Department of the Environment booklets (as at May 1989)

1 The Tenants' Charter (being revised)
2. Right To Repair (available)
3. The Rent Acts and You (discontinued)
4. Letting Rooms in Your Home (discontinued, but revised as 22)
5. Letting Your Home or Retirement Home (discontinued)
6. Controlled Tenancies (discontinued)
7. Regulated Tenancies (discontinued, but revised as 25)
8. Shorthold: 2nd Revision (discontinued)
9. Leasehold Reform (available)
10. Service Charges in Flats (discontinued, but revised as 27)
11. Notice to Quit (discontinued, but revised as 24)
12. Wanting to Move? (available)
13. Housing Association Rents (discontinued)
14. Home Improvement Grants (available)
15. Local Authority Shared Ownership (available)
16. Mobile Homes (available, but to be revised)
17. Assured Tenancies (Housing Act 1980) (discontinued)
18. Housing Defects (available)
19. Assured Tenancies (Housing Act 1988) (available)
20. Repairs (new, forthcoming)
21. "He Wants Me Out": Harassment (available)
22. Letting Rooms in Your Home (new, revised no.4, available)
23. Agricultural Lettings (new, forthcoming)
24. Notice That You Must Leave (new, revised no.11, forthcoming)
25. Regulated Tenancies (new, revised no.7, available)
26. The Rights and Duties of Landlords and Tenants of Houses (available)
27. Management of Flats — The Rights and Duties of Landlords and Tenants (new, replaces no.10, forthcoming)
28. Right of First Refusal (available)
29. A Guide for the Tenants of Housing Associations (new, forthcoming)

A number of associated booklets, either available or planned-
● Houses Held on Ground Lease (available)
● Redemption of Rent Charges (available)
● Apportionment of Rents (available)

- Tenants' Choice (new, forthcoming)
- Community Charge and Rent (new, forthcoming)
- Lodgers (new, forthcoming)

All of these booklets can be obtained free, in bulk, from:-

DoE Leaflets Central Stores
Building No.3
Victoria Road
South Ruislip
HA4 ONZ

Index